The Tender Heart

The Tender Heart

CONQUERING

YOUR

INSECURITY

Joseph Nowinski, Ph.D.

A Fireside Book
Published by Simon & Schuster
New York London Toronto
Sydney Singapore

FIRESIDE
Rockefeller Center
1230 Avenue of the Americas
New York, NY 10020

Designed by Elina D. Nudelman

Manufactured in the United States of America

10   9   8   7   6   5   4   3   2   1

Library of Congress Cataloging-in-Publication Data is available.

ISBN 0-684-87167-X

For Rebecca Jane Nowinski

Contents

The Tender Heart

Prologue

Have you ever been called thin-skinned?

Do you get jealous easily?

Are you a self-conscious person?

Can even a minor conflict with someone close to you send you into an emotional tailspin, clouding your mood and outlook for days?

Does even slight criticism trigger feelings of anxiety or depression that distract you and linger?

Do you find it hard to be direct with people, for fear of hurting their feelings or making them angry?

Have you often felt let down, even by those you are closest to?

Do you live with constant, nagging worries that somehow you just don't measure up?

Have you ever felt that you were emotionally manipulated by someone who took advantage of your sensitive nature?

If one or more of the above questions describes you or someone you love, then this book could help.

The Tender Heart is about how certain personality traits are formed, specifically *insecurity*. This term has been popular for a long time; probably most of us have used it to describe either ourselves or someone we know. Yet as often as it is used, the concept of insecurity is not well understood.

This book is about insecurity: what it is, where it comes from, and how to conquer it. *The Tender Heart* will enable you to understand the nature and causes of insecurity, and what you can do to heal it in yourself. You will learn how to watch out for insecurity as it affects your behavior and daily outlook, and you will discover how to minimize the negative effects that insecurity can have on your personal life, as well as your work life. If you are a parent, you will learn what you can do to prevent insecurity in your children.

Insecurity robs us of our zest for life. Instead of approaching life with openness and excitement, insecurity makes us approach life in a defensive, self-conscious, and anxious way. It undermines our potential for success, and it smothers our creativity. Insecurity makes true intimacy difficult if not impossible to achieve, and limits a relationship's growth.

The good news is that insecurity *can* be overcome. It is definitely *not* the equivalent of a psychological life sentence. Inside every insecure personality lies a sensitive soul. It is very possible for the insecure man or woman to shed insecurity and free that soul.

Loss and separation, and conflict or criticism, can affect some people so severely that they become dysfunctional. Their *insecurity* can seriously compromise these men and women's capacity to successfully form and sustain relationships and fulfill their potential. They tend to be chronic underachievers—in love as much as in the workplace. Many of these people were born *sensitive;* but they were *not* born insecure; rather, they *became* insecure as a result of their experiences. Perhaps you—or someone you love—is like this. Perhaps you or they have experienced the pain of having extreme and dysfunctional reactions to conflict, criticism, or loss. Perhaps you have experienced what it is like to have been born sensitive, and then to have become insecure.

***

This book looks at the way in which the type of *dispositions* we are born with interacts with the *experiences* we have to determine the unique *personality* we eventually develop. People may be born sensitive, but they are not born insecure. That means there is much that can be done to heal insecurity in ourselves. It also means that parents can help prevent insecurity from undermining even the most sensitive of children's potential to find fulfilling relationships and realize their potential. This book will also help you to understand why some people are especially vulnerable in relationships and get hurt easily and often, and why there are some people who have trouble ever being intimate, and who are pretty much unaffected when a relationship ends.

Insecurity plays a major role in the way people view the world and in how they respond to it, including how people react to conflict, criticism, and loss. For example, consider the different ways in which people react to a loss, such as the loss of a relationship. Most of us are familiar with the idea that people go through several stages of grief when they experience such a loss. The grief process is said to start with *denial:* refusing to face the facts of a loss. We may, for example, tell ourselves something like, "He didn't really mean it when he said he wanted to break up," or, "I'll just call him tomorrow—he'll feel better by then."

From denial, grief progresses to *bargaining,* which can look something like this: "Maybe he just needs a little space. I'll give him some space and then he'll decide he still wants us to be together." Another common variation on bargaining is to decide that dating others is really okay, and that it doesn't mean the relationship is really over.

When denial breaks down and bargaining fails, grief progresses to *anger.* We are, understandably, angry about losing our boyfriend or girlfriend, husband or wife. Beneath this anger, though, lies a lot of *pain and sadness,* which mark the next stage in the grief process.

The final stage is called, simply, *acceptance.* At this point there may be some lingering sadness, or at least moments of sadness; but there is no more denial or bargaining, and our anger and pain have largely subsided.

Grief typically does not follow these stages so neatly. It is, rather, a process, and we can move back and forth between stages for some time as we work our way from denial to acceptance. Still, although these stages may accurately describe normal, or average, grief, most of us also know that people's reactions to loss in reality vary a great deal—so much so that we might question whether these stages, and the normal grief process, truly apply to everyone. Reactions to loss can differ so drastically that, observing them, it can be hard at times to make sense of some of them. Consider the following three different reactions to the breakup of a relationship.

The first person reacts to the breakup with a deep feeling of sadness that waxes and wanes. At times he cries, or at least feels like crying. Seeking comfort, he turns to the company of old and trusted friends. He may be distracted, sleep poorly, or find that his appetite is gone. He wonders at times whether the breakup couldn't somehow have been avoided if either he or his ex had only done something differently. Regardless of the reasons for the breakup, there are moments when he misses his ex-partner, and at these times feelings of sadness dominate his mood. There are moments, too, when he is just plain mad at her for leaving him.

This first person is experiencing grief, to be sure. He feels sad, lonely, even angry or regretful at times. However, he does not feel suicidal or overly guilt-ridden. He definitely does not hate himself, feel panicked, or think he is worthless. He continues to function fairly well, and as far as the future is concerned, he feels far from hopeless.

The second person's reaction couldn't be more different. This one can be difficult to comprehend. Judging from the way he acts and what he has to say, it's difficult to tell that this person has experienced a loss at all. As best you can tell he doesn't appear to be suffering in the least as a result of the breakup—and he doesn't seem to be pretending, or putting on a good face. His life goes on, seemingly without missing a beat. If the subject of the lost relationship comes up, he shrugs it off, showing little if any feeling. If he talks about the breakup at all, his attitude is that it was entirely the other person's fault. And if pressed to talk about it, the only emotion he shows is anger—not about the breakup, but at you for pressuring him to talk about it. He reveals neither sorrow nor regret; nor does he take any personal responsibility for what went wrong, or have a kind word to say about his ex-partner. If anything, he puts his ex down, going so far as to disclose personal things that most people would keep private. He appears ready to move on to another relationship immediately, almost as if the one that just ended had never existed. Most important, he doesn't believe there is anything he did that contributed to the breakup; nor does he wish that he'd done anything differently. As far as he is concerned, the ex-partner and the relationship they had together are little more than last week's news.

The third person takes the breakup extremely hard. He sinks into a deep depression and is overcome by profound and persistent feelings of emptiness and hopelessness. His lingering depression is punctuated, though, by moments when his sadness gives way to resentment and anger over being rejected, as well as more than a little self-pity. He feels that his ex let him down, and that he was a fool to trust her—or anyone else for that matter—in the first place. In general he is preoccupied with the loss and can't get his ex-partner out of his mind. He spends hour after hour ruminating, holding on tenaciously to both his sadness and his resentment. In his mind he goes over, again and again, the entire history of the relationship, combing his memory for every little fight, every hurt feeling, and obsessing over what he or his ex could or should have done differently. On some level the breakup seems incomprehensible to him, the reality of it too overwhelming to bear. His distraction and obsession is so intense that it interferes with the rest of his life. He loses efficiency at work. He loses sleep, loses weight. He starts drinking more, and thinks about asking his doctor for medication to help him cope with his unbearable sense of despair. Friends try to comfort him, only to find that he is inconsolable.

***

What accounts for why these people react to the same kind of loss in such dramatically different ways?

Differences in *personality* account for this variation in response to loss. We each possess a unique personality, which is the outcome of the dispositions we are born with plus the experiences we have had. What many people would like to know (and what they need to know in order to understand and help themselves) is precisely *what* combination of disposition and experience can explain such profoundly different personalities, and therefore such vastly different responses. Only by knowing the answer to that question can people take action to prevent themselves (or others) from experiencing the kind of debilitating reaction that the third person had. Only by knowing that can we understand what exactly is going on inside the second person, who seems to have no reaction—no *heart* at all. This is the key to understanding not only the different ways that people grieve but also why some people cannot be intimate or experience love in the way we commonly think of it, whereas others seem destined to fall in love easily and have their hearts broken time and time again.

In an effort to explain the behavior of the second person described above, some people might be tempted to write it off by arguing that people like that are in denial about their loss. This thinking is based on the assumption that a person couldn't *truly* feel so little about the loss of a close relationship. Or could they? Surely they must be avoiding dealing with it. Although tempting, this explanation is often wrong. In fact, this book will explain why such a reaction can be exactly what it appears to be.

Similar differences between people can be observed in how they react not only to loss but to conflict and criticism as well. Understanding these differences, and what can be done to minimize the most severe ones, and what we need to know about those who seem relatively unaffected by loss (and who may be turned on by conflict), is also the subject of this book.

***

The Tender Heart aims to provide meaningful explanations and practical solutions to men and women who are thin-skinned, self-conscious, and prone to severe depression in response to loss and separation, to relatively minor conflicts, and to the kinds of criticism that we are all bound to encounter. These kinds of reactions relate to two factors. The first is the *nature of the traumas we have experienced* in our lives, and the stage of development we were at when we experienced them. Traumatic experiences include major losses, such as the divorce of our parents, the early death of a parent, physical or sexual abuse, and severe neglect. But more subtle things, such as frequent separations from those we are attached to, as well as rejection by them and their indifference toward us, can also be traumatic for some, especially for those who are naturally sensitive. For example, an indifferent parent who expresses little if any interest in a child and is neither affectionate nor nurturing can create insecurity in a sensitive child just as surely as a parent who physically abuses a child. Similarly, in a sensitive child, a life marked by continual change and chaos can be enough to create insecurity.

* * *

The second factor that determines whether we will become insecure is the type of *disposition* we are born with. Depending on how severe they are and when they happen, some losses have the potential to affect almost all of us in very negative ways. Certain traumatic experiences, in other words, have the potential to make most of us at least a little insecure. More typically, though, experience in and of itself does not entirely account for insecurity. If it did, then everyone who's been exposed to some loss or abuse would be equally insecure, and we know this is not the case.

What you could call people's natural temperament—something that is part of our biological inheritance—consists of a series of dispositions. As any mother of more than one child can tell you, there are clear differences between the dispositions children are born with. Some children are hesitant or curious, gregarious or shy, active or sedentary almost from birth. For most of history the idea of innate dispositions, and of people being born with different temperaments, has been accepted in most cultures as a simple fact of life. It is reflected in some of our greatest novels about families and family life. In this century, though, this idea had lost favor in some circles, particularly among those who would like to believe that personality is infinitely malleable and that it has everything to do with experience, nothing to do with nature.

Among the dispositions we are born with is one that I call *interpersonal sensitivity.* It is a part of one's biological inheritance, just as much as hair color and bone structure. Many people I've worked with are very obviously *tenderhearted* and have been that way for as long as they can remember. They always reacted more to loss and separation than others did, even as children. They always had an exceptional ability to understand what others were feeling, and were themselves easily moved to tears or laughter. They also were prone to avoid intense conflict, and would hesitate to do anything that might hurt someone else's feelings. In general they always experienced all of their own emotions very deeply. As adults they continue to be more tenderhearted and sensitive than most.

In contrast, there are those among us who could accurately be called *tough-hearted*. Like their tenderhearted counterparts, these people too have always been that way. Their innate dispositions, though, are the exact opposite of the tenderhearted. They are a lot less interpersonally sensitive. They do not empathize with others as well as tenderhearted people do; neither do they experience their own feelings as deeply. They are less hesitant to get into conflict, and they can be brusque.

A common mistake that is made by tenderhearted people—and one that can be very costly to them—is to fail to recognize or to accept this reality. Instead, many tenderhearted people are inclined to believe that everyone else is just like them, and they are often surprised and confused when they encounter someone who seems insensitive, lacking in empathy, or willing to hurt others without a second thought. Once committed to a relationship with a toughhearted person, a tenderhearted soul may cling for years to the belief that she will someday change her insensitive partner, if only she tries hard enough or loves him enough. The truth, though, is that tenderhearted people in these situations may be more likely to be exploited or abused than to change their insensitive partners. In the extreme, some tough-hearted types feed off sensitive people, satisfying their own appetites and leaving their tenderhearted victims drained.

You can benefit by applying the information here not just to yourself but also to your partner, and even to your work and family relationships. However, you must accept that people are born with certain dispositions and the idea that these traits can predispose some to becoming insecure. Differences in interpersonal sensitivity can play a decisive role in our long-term success or failure, including our success in relationships.

***

Some of the ideas in this book—such as the notion that there are *emotional predators,* and that these men and women can and often do prey on the tenderhearted—might arouse discomfort or even protest. Yet I believe that by understanding these concepts you can enhance your relationships and avoid the emotional pain of getting into ones that are likely to lead only to frustration and heartache. If you are the parent of a tenderhearted child, you can develop your child's sensitivity while helping him not to succumb to insecurity.

1

Insecurity

Perhaps you know someone who reacted severely—to the point where it struck you as irrational or pathological—to the loss of a relationship. Perhaps you know someone who gets deeply depressed or feels unnecessarily betrayed in response to the slightest criticism. Maybe you yourself tend to react this way. Then again, maybe you are one of those people whose heart gets broken more often than seems fair, or who is drawn to exactly the wrong kind of person—one who is insensitive and inevitably hurts you.

The intense reactions associated with a dysfunctional response to loss, rejection, or criticism are the result of *insecurity*. Insecurity may mean different things to different people. In general, though, whenever I ask people for their impressions, they typically associate insecurity with someone who is constantly second-guessing himself, whose feelings are easily hurt, and who seeks continual reassurance. These commonsense definitions accurately capture the essence of insecurity.

In this book the word *insecurity* has a particular meaning, and a particular cause. Insecurity refers to a profound sense of self-doubt—a deep feeling of uncertainty about our basic worth and our place in the world. Insecurity is associated with chronic self-consciousness, along with a chronic lack of confidence in ourselves and anxiety about our relationships. The insecure man or woman lives in constant fear of rejection and a deep uncertainty about whether his or her own feelings and desires are legitimate. In men as well as women, insecurity comes from a combination of a sensitive disposition and experiences of loss, abuse, rejection, or neglect. However, while insecurity has the same causes in men and women, outwardly men and women usually express insecurity in different ways.

The insecure person also harbors unrealistic expectations about love and relationships. These expectations, for themselves and for others, are often unconscious. The insecure person creates a situation in which being disappointed and hurt in relationships is almost inevitable. Ironically, although insecure people are easily and frequently hurt, they are usually unaware of how they are unwitting accomplices in creating their own misery.

Although the two can be related, insecurity is *not* the same as sensitivity. It's entirely possible, in other words, to be sensitive but not insecure. In fact, one goal of this book is to give parents guidance in how to foster sensitivity in their children without creating insecurity. Another goal is to help insecure people shed their insecurity without sacrificing their sensitivity. We'll be looking much closer at what kinds of experiences tend to make an interpersonally sensitive person vulnerable to becoming insecure, what kind of experiences can make insecurity worse, and what kinds of experiences can help to heal it.

HOW INSECURE AM I?

This is a question that most people would like an answer to. Since most of us can relate to the idea of being insecure sometimes, the bigger issue is just how much insecurity is an issue in our lives. You can begin to find the answer by assessing your own level of insecurity (or that of someone you love) as it is right now. To do this, complete the following questionnaire by checking off all statements that describe you (or your loved one).

Insecurity Inventory
_____ I often worry about my relationship.

_____ I do not like being in the spotlight socially.

_____ I often feel that others don't take me seriously.

_____ I am an exceptionally jealous person.

_____ I'm forever thinking that others are smarter, more attractive, or more interesting than me.

_____ I worry that my partner is going to leave me for someone else.

_____ I would describe myself as very self-conscious.

_____ I've been told that I'm thin-skinned, overly sensitive.

_____ I often seek other people's approval, even if I don't particularly respect them.

_____ I've been told by friends and partners that I expect too much from myself and others.

_____ If someone hurts my feelings I have a hard time letting go of it and tend to dwell on it for a long time.

_____ I am very hard on myself when I make a mistake.

_____ I often ask my partner for reassurance that she/he still loves me.

_____ I get either angry or depressed if someone I care about disappoints me.

_____ I cry easily.

_____ I am very sensitive to criticism.

_____ I worry about how I look.

_____ I have a hard time trusting my partner not to cheat on me.

_____ I have a strong desire to make amends whenever I do or say something that seems to hurt someone else.

_____ I'm more inclined to think too little than too much of myself.

_____ Sometimes I feel anxious for no apparent reason.

_____ I worry about being disapproved of.

_____ I've been told that I'm very defensive if I'm criticized even slightly.

_____ I have often felt let down by people, even the ones who love me.

_____ I secretly feel that I'm not smart enough or attractive enough.

_____ I sometimes worry that even my best friends don't really like me.

_____ Most of the time I would sooner give in than fight for what I want.

_____ My feelings are easily hurt.

_____ If I do something that gets my partner angry I have a hard time getting it out of my mind.

_____ I often don't have confidence in decisions I make.

_____ It really bothers me when I think someone doesn't like me.

_____ If someone hurts my feelings I am more likely to give them the cold shoulder than to confront them.

_____ I often make up excuses rather just telling the truth.

_____ I worry more than most people about what other people think of me.

_____ I will do almost anything to avoid conflicts with others.

The more items you checked off, the more likely it is that the person you are rating—either yourself or someone you love—is insecure.

It's important to understand that insecurity is not something that a person either has or doesn't have, period. Just as people's reactions to loss (or abuse or rejection) can vary, people can differ a great deal in how insecure they are. There is no sharp boundary line separating those of us who are secure from those who are *in*secure. Few if any of us could say that we have never experienced any symptoms of insecurity. Most of us have some degree of sensitivity, and most of us have experienced at least some significant losses or separations, abuse, or rejection in our lives. On the other hand, not all of us have reacted to these experiences by becoming intensely insecure. The issue, then, is not whether any of us has any insecurity, but rather how severe and debilitating our insecurity is.

Human beings seem programmed to form attachments—to people, places, even things. The more sensitive we are by nature, the more this is true. One route to insecurity is through experiencing broken attachments. In general, the more significant the attachment is and the younger we are when it happens, the more a broken attachment affects us. This is all the more true for those who are sensitive by nature. Attachments can be broken by physical separation, as when a parent dies or our parents divorce. They can also be broken through abuse or neglect. It's important to keep in mind that children experience emotional coldness, physical abuse, and chronic criticism as *loss,* just as surely as they experience physical separation that way.

When they think about broken attachments, most people think about very young children who are either separated from their parents or abused. These kinds of experiences do place young children at risk for becoming insecure. It's also true that broken attachments throughout childhood and adolescence have the potential to create insecurity.

In contrast, while losses can affect us as adults, they typically don't create insecurity in a person who is not already insecure. The most vulnerable period for the development of insecurity, then, is childhood.

Few of us could say we have never suffered the loss of an attachment, or experienced at least some of the symptoms of insecurity. Who has not experienced at least a little hesitancy or distrust following the breakup of an important relationship? And how many people can honestly say that they've never had their hearts broken? The exceptions—people who cannot relate to such experiences—turn out to be people whom we need to watch out for, and avoid getting into relationships with, if possible.

If insecurity is to some extent unavoidable, then the key question becomes this: at what point does insecurity become dysfunctional? I believe that when insecurity is so intense and lasting that it seriously undermines our self-esteem and interferes with our ability to enjoy life, to build and keep satisfying relationships, and to achieve our career potential, it is dysfunctional. At that point the insecure person has a distorted self-image and lacks a sense of their place and value in the world. At that point insecurity leads us to harbor totally unrealistic expectations for relationships, or else leads us to choose partners who use or abuse us. At that point insecurity definitely *is* dysfunctional, and at that point it is worth doing something about. *In fact, if that kind of insecurity is not identified and addressed, sooner or later it can and will cause us great pain, sabotage our potential for success, and very likely destroy our relationships.*

This leads us to a second question: how can insecurity be overcome? First, we must be able to recognize insecurity for what it is and to see how it has affected us. It helps a great deal in overcoming insecurity to understand how it has roots both in our disposition and in our experiences.

Insecurity operates in strange and varied ways. It can sometimes lurk beneath the surface for a long time, even in a seemingly healthy individual, until some experience comes along to set it off, often with disastrous results.

Peter and Helen, both forty-eight, made an appointment to see me because, as Peter explained over the phone, he was feeling angry. Though his tone of voice was mild, Peter's words were not. "It's intense," he explained, referring to his anger. "I just can't get past it. I've been feeling this way for nearly a year, and it's at the point where we—or I should say I—am seriously considering separating."

The urgency I sensed in Peter's voice made me decide to meet with him and Helen two days later. Then, when I met with them, I found myself wondering why I'd sensed that urgency. From the moment they sat down I was impressed with the respect and consideration they showed each other. I had expected tension and stress, but all I saw was a couple whose gentleness was the most striking feature of their relationship. Even when Peter brought up the subject of his anger and spoke of separation, his regard for Helen was plain.

I wasn't sure what to make of what I was seeing. Caught off guard, I just sat back, invited them to talk, and listened.

I listened for half an hour as Helen and Peter described the history of a twenty-six-year marriage and a family life that most would consider not just satisfactory but downright enviable. Both professionals and both attractive and fit, they told the story of a marriage in which they had managed to support each other's careers at the same time that they'd raised two children, both of whom were now college educated and gainfully employed. They described their family as close, and it was apparent from the way they spoke, and from the expressions on their faces, that Peter and Helen shared a deep sense of pride in their children. When I asked them how many of their twenty-six years together had been happy ones, they immediately agreed on the answer: "All but one," said Peter. "The last one."

Why would this couple, whose relationship seemed so blessed for so long and who regarded each other with such obvious respect, rather suddenly be contemplating separating? What was I missing? There had to be something hidden. Had one of them suddenly committed some unforgivable offense that hadn't yet been mentioned?

Regardless of what I didn't know, one thing was pretty clear to me: this was a marriage between two *interpersonally sensitive,* or *tenderhearted,* people. What I didn't know then, though, was that one of them was not just sensitive but also very *insecure*. From our first session on it was evident that Peter, despite the resentments he expressed, remained sensitive to Helen and cared for her. And despite her anguish at the prospect of separation, Helen clearly cared a great deal for Peter and was able to identify with his feelings. Insensitive people don't relate to others in this way. They don't put themselves in someone else's shoes and know what the other person is feeling or wanting. If anything, they are focused on their own needs and desires. Unlike Peter, when an insensitive man is angry he doesn't particularly care about how that anger impacts another person. In certain extreme cases he can find conflict not uncomfortable but actually exciting. This description, though, fit neither Helen nor Peter.

I asked Peter and Helen to explain to me what had brought about the sudden downturn in their relationship, and braced myself to hear some secret not yet revealed. I shared with them my perception that they treated each other with affection and respect. They both smiled, which only added to my sense that the idea of this couple separating was bizarre indeed.

Peter looked over at Helen, who nodded her approval. Then he spoke in words carefully chosen. "Well," he said, "the problem is that for about the last year or so Helen has been, in my opinion at least, extremely angry, and also extremely critical of me. She was never that way before. On the contrary, she's always been an incredibly supportive and nurturing person. But to tell you the truth, the past year has been hell. It's like she's become a different person."

For the first time, Peter's voice began to show a trace of anger; but just a trace. "I know it may not seem that way from the outside," he said, seeming to know very well how he came across, "but the truth is that on the inside I'm incredibly angry at Helen. I'm so angry that I believe my feelings for her have changed. I just feel that I don't want to be her husband anymore."

I looked over at Helen. There were tears in her eyes. Our eyes met. I waited for her to talk. "It's true," she said, an embarrassed smile on her face. "Peter's right. I have been very different for the past year or so. I've been critical and impatient a lot of the time. And I've lost my temper on any number of occasions, for no good reason. I seem to have become a very intolerant person. There are times when I'm so frustrated that I feel like I'm going to explode. I can't understand why. And Peter's right, too, that I've directed a lot of this at him. I've said things I regret, but the damage, I suppose, is done. And one thing that Peter is not saying is that I've also lost all my interest in sex. Lost it totally. We always had a very good sex life—at least I thought so—but that's gone now, too."

"What have you been critical about?" I asked Helen.

She sighed. "Oh, just about everything," she said. "You name it. I seem to have suddenly become unhappy with the very qualities that attracted me to Peter—things like his soft-spoken manner, his neatness, his punctuality. I've no idea why, but this past year I seem to have found virtually everything about Peter intolerable at one time or another."

Peter nodded in response to what Helen said. In a gesture of support he reached out and touched her arm. This was too much for me. "It's painfully obvious to me," I said, "that you two still have a great deal of affection and regard for each other. Frankly, you seem to me to be in love with each other. I'm puzzled as to why you'd want to separate."

Peter breathed a sigh. "I do have a lot of regard for Helen," he said. "But I also feel betrayed by her. I don't trust her anymore. I still like her, but I'm not sure she likes or respects me. And there's definitely a part of me that's angry, that wants to hurt her, and that wants to leave."

Helen spoke next. "I can definitely feel Peter's anger and resentment," she said. "Even though he might not seem that way to you, I know he's angry. And I know he feels betrayed by me. I believe him when he says that he feels that he has to separate from me."

As I started to overcome my own incredulity at what I was witnessing, I decided that the only thing to do was to take what Helen and Peter were saying at face value, as puzzling as it was, and to try to understand why it was that Peter felt compelled to take such strong action as to separate from Helen over the sorts of things she'd admitted saying and doing. After all, at least from where I sat, she was still a committed, concerned, and supportive spouse.

It had already occurred to me that the behaviors that Helen was describing—irritability, loss of interest in sex, mood swings—were all symptoms of clinical depression, and I offered this as a hypothesis. As educated as they were, it seemed that this possibility had not occurred to either of them. Helen had wondered if she was going through menopause. Peter, meanwhile, had wondered if his wife simply had grown tired of marriage or lost her attraction to him. What to me was an alternative but obvious explanation—that Helen had fallen victim to a midlife depression—was a totally novel idea to them.

I decided to refer Helen to a colleague for evaluation of her depression and to see Peter individually a few times. I suggested that we all get together after that, in about a month. I did not attempt to talk them out of separating, although I did suggest that waiting one month did not seem unreasonable. Something in his expression told me Peter would not take my advice.

When Peter met with me the next week, I learned that he indeed had not taken my advice. On the contrary, he and Helen had done some apartment shopping together over the weekend. They'd found an inexpensive studio apartment located over an old carriage house. It was clean and bright, and (most important) available immediately, and Peter rented it on the spot. Helen helped him sort through their vast collection of pots and pans, old furniture, and linens, and together they'd come up with more than enough essentials to furnish the place. Then Helen helped Peter move in!

I shook my head and told Peter that this was the most amiable separation I'd ever heard of. Then I asked him how Helen was doing. He acknowledged that she was upset. But she was also trying hard, he said, to respect his decision. I asked whether they'd argued at all over what he could take from the house. He smiled and said they'd had a few words over a favorite old coffeepot, but he'd quickly relented and left it at the house. Anything else? I asked. Peter nodded. There had also been some tension, he said, over the issue of whether he should have free access to the house after he'd left. It hadn't crossed his mind that this might be an issue, and it surprised him when Helen told him that she did not want him to come over without calling first. It wasn't that she had anything to hide, she said; rather, she simply wanted to avoid having to live in anticipation of whether Peter might show up at any moment.

Then I asked Peter how *he* was feeling. "Sad," he replied. "But basically I think this was the right thing to do. I mean, I feel I *had* to do it." I didn't argue. Instead, I turned my attention to trying to find out what it was about Peter's personality and personal history that might account for his actions, which still struck me as extreme. I shared my impression with him, explaining that what he'd done seemed to me to be something of a payback: a settling of a score of some kind. As best I could tell, I said, Peter seemed driven to hurt Helen, perhaps in retaliation for the way he'd been hurt by her. Judging by his actions, I imagined she must have hurt him very badly. But exactly *how* she had hurt him was not clear to me, I said.

Peter nodded. Helen's actions *had* hurt him badly, he said, and my idea that he somehow needed to strike back also struck him as on the mark. He confessed that at times the intensity of his urge to hurt Helen seemed out of proportion even to himself. As he described it, the feeling ran deep. "It's also totally out of character for me," he explained, "to walk around feeling this rage just bubbling beneath the surface. I think it's fair to say that most people who know me would say that I'm definitely not the raging or vindictive type."

I explained to Peter that I believed that there are real differences between people in terms of how interpersonally sensitive they are. Some people fall on the *tenderhearted* end of this dimension, most fall somewhere in the middle, and others still could best be described as *tough-hearted*. Peter agreed. He also agreed that both he and Helen definitely fell well over on the tenderhearted end of the interpersonal-sensitivity dimension.

As evidence of his own sensitivity, Peter described how his feelings were deeply hurt when Helen first began to become irritable and critical. "It sent me into an absolute depression," he said. "Even the mildest impatience on her part, or the most casual critical comment, would send me into a tailspin. I know you're probably thinking that I'm overly sensitive, but I can't help it. It was like Helen was rejecting the very heart of the person I am. Sometimes her criticism and anger weren't so mild, either."

I asked Peter to give me an example of one of Helen's worst criticisms. It didn't take him long to respond, and he blushed with anger just thinking about it. "She told me more than once to 'toughen up.' Those were her exact words."

"What were they in response to?" I asked.

"She said that when I complained about some other comment she'd made. That was just so out of character for her. I mean, she knows that I pride myself on being a reasonable, rational person. I go out of my way to avoid hurting others' feelings. I don't *want* to become 'tough.'"

Peter could not recall ever feeling so bad. Up until then—through virtually all of their courtship and marriage—Helen had been nothing but a loving, accommodating, and supportive partner. Of course, they'd had their disagreements over the years, he said; but these were surprisingly rare and always seemed to get resolved with an absolute minimum of confrontation, and virtually no hostility.

Though I am no advocate of conflict, I've always believed that there is something healthy about learning to deal with differences, and to manage them without resorting to abuse in one form or another. In some ways Peter's marriage as he described it came across as too good to be true, and I said so. I wondered out loud if he realized how unusual and exceptional his marriage had been all these years, and how it might have been a mixed blessing in that it had pretty much insulated Peter from conflict. Peter appreciated my point. Friends had made similar comments at times, he said, to both him and Helen over the years.

Could it be, I then asked, that Peter had been so blessed in this marriage that he'd developed unrealistic expectations about what long-term relationships were really like? Alternatively, could he have had such expectations all along, but been lucky enough to have found a partner who could actually fulfill them?

Peter thought, then nodded again, but said he didn't know if either of those possibilities was really true. I pushed ahead. Had Peter considered, I asked, that he might be being excessively harsh and judgmental in deciding that what could be nothing more than symptoms of depression in his wife warranted the extreme measure of separation? This time Peter shrugged. Maybe, he said, shifting in his chair, but he still felt that he had to leave.

So, you might ask, was Peter crazy? Not really. Not, at least, in any clinical sense, though some might say he was crazy to consider walking away from a wife like Helen. I could tell, however, from the way he'd reacted to my slightly challenging questions that Peter was a man who did not like to be challenged or criticized. And clearly he also had unrealistic expectations for his relationship with Helen—expectations that I suspected he hadn't developed since being with Helen but had brought into the relationship twenty-six years earlier.

Peter's unrealistic expectations had revealed themselves as soon as Helen started to show even the slightest impatience or criticism, or to withhold affection. Peter's reaction to these changes was immediate and intense. Until then you could say that he'd been pretty much insulated from his own insecurity, at least in his marriage, by the fact that Helen had always been such a caring, affectionate, and considerate wife. She essentially met his expectations, unrealistic or not. Conflict and criticism had been such a rare event in this marriage that the soft underside of Peter's personality had never been exposed. Knowing that, I also knew there had to be more to Peter's history than I had heard so far.

Having established that Peter and Helen were both sensitive, tenderhearted people, I now began to suspect, based on our discussion, that Peter was not just sensitive but insecure as well. In fact, the more Peter described himself and Helen, the more apparent it became that he had many telltale signs of fairly severe insecurity. For example, despite considerable success, both professionally and financially, he had always suffered from a nagging feeling that he hadn't done well enough—that his colleagues were brighter, more creative, more recognized than he. He described himself as an exceedingly self-conscious and shy individual, so much so that this had held him back from pursuing several opportunities for advancement, as well as offices in professional organizations. "Most people would say that I've been pretty successful," he confided. "But I've also stayed in place for many years, instead of moving ahead. I've watched some of my colleagues—especially the more aggressive ones—go after and get positions in our professional organization, grants, even awards, by pushing for them. I see myself as having done a good job, but not really going after success or recognition the way they do."

Peter knew himself well enough to admit that he was exceedingly sensitive to criticism, and he even acknowledged that this was a big reason why the change in Helen had been so hard on him. He felt he did a better job of hiding his feelings at the workplace, but still, whenever a colleague questioned anything he did, no matter how mildly, he'd ruminate about it for days. But even here Peter had been fortunate; because he was talented, he was rarely subject to very much criticism at all, and so his insecurity had never surfaced in full force, at least not until the past year.

As Peter and I reflected together on the history of his relationship with Helen, he volunteered the observation that he'd always sought approval and praise from her, much more so than she did from him. "She's always seemed comfortable with herself," he said, "while I don't think I've ever felt that way about myself."

Peter, I also learned, suffered from severe self-doubts, not just about his success and his competence but also about his physical attractiveness. He'd always thought he was too short and too thin, and that he had a goofy smile. He'd not had his first date until college, partly because he was too insecure to pursue women. Even after he met Helen, in their junior year, and felt fairly certain that she liked him, he hesitated. It was she who arranged for their first date, inviting him to be her escort at a formal dinner dance she'd been invited to.

As the pieces of the picture began to come together, I felt more and more certain that it was Peter's insecurity that was playing the key role in what was going on now between him and Helen. What was still missing, though, was an understanding of what kind of experiences in his past had so wounded this sensitive man that he became as insecure as he was. The answer turned out to lie in his relationships with his parents.

"We were raised by my father," Peter said. His tone of voice, I noticed, had suddenly become hard, harder even than it had been when we were talking about Helen's criticizing him. That and the suddenly stony expression on his face clearly suggested some intense underlying feelings.

"Who's 'we'"? I asked.

"There was me and my sister," he replied. "She's five years younger than me."

What was bringing up all these emotions? Had his parents divorced? Was his father abusive? Had his mother been ill or otherwise unavailable? I asked Peter to tell me more.

He frowned. "No, she wasn't 'ill,'" he replied sarcastically. "Not unless you call being chronically unfaithful an illness. She would come around once, sometimes twice a week. You'd never know when. She'd stay long enough to cook a meal, maybe do a wash. Then she'd disappear again."

"Where did she go?" I asked.

"Out. With other guys."

"You're saying that she was unfaithful?"

Peter nodded, a wry smile on his face. Then he looked me square in the eyes. "That's one way of saying it. Another way is that she had more boyfriends than you could count."

"Your father suspected this?" I asked.

That smile flashed again. "Suspected? He more than suspected. It was obvious he knew. He just kept quiet, though I could see it ate him up. Eventually he became sick, then developed a heart problem. If he'd taken care of himself, I'm certain he could have lived longer. But he didn't take care of himself, and he died at the age of fifty-five."

"Your parents—they stayed together despite the infidelity?"

Peter nodded, and again I asked him to tell me more.

Apparently, not long after marrying Peter's father, his mother had decided that she didn't love the man. Yet she didn't leave. On the contrary, she went on to have a second child by him; and as far as Peter knew, although his parents didn't live together for some fifteen years before his father died, they had never divorced or even legally separated.

For as long as he could remember, Peter's mother had actively and fairly openly pursued other relationships. To make matters worse, she occasionally took Peter along when she would visit her latest friend. "I really hated that," Peter said.

Peter also described his mother as fickle. "It's like the old rhyme: when she was good, she was very good, but when she was bad, she was horrid. That's how she was: loving one minute, cold as ice the next. She could really bring you down if she wanted to. Her tongue was sharper than any knife. I saw my father get cut down by her plenty of times. Eventually he just avoided her, and they lived pretty much separate lives."

Although Peter loved his father deeply and respected him for taking on the dual role of breadwinner and parent, Peter was almost as angry at his father as he was at his mother. Why? For failing to divorce her. Peter could not abide his father's decision to stay in a marriage that Peter himself felt humiliated by. "To this day I don't know how he could have done it," he said, his disgust evident.

The picture now came into full focus, not only for me but, as he spoke, I thought, for Peter as well. Before my eyes his whole demeanor changed. Emotions that had been buried within him for years suddenly flowed to the surface, then erupted. Defenses he'd built against his pain gave way. His face went slack, and then he cried.

At that moment it became painfully clear to both of us why Peter had been acting as he had—not only why he'd felt compelled to act decisively (as his father never had) and separate from Helen, but also why he was hurt so deeply and driven to hurt her in return. It was payback, all right; but Helen not only was paying for her own actions—she was paying for Peter's mother's actions, and for his father's inaction as well.

Peter had always been a sensitive man; in fact, Helen said that she'd been attracted to Peter precisely because of that sensitivity. He was kind and considerate, contributed generously to charities, and went out of his way to settle disagreements without resorting to anger. She'd always appreciated her husband's gentleness and had surprised herself when she started finding these qualities in him irritating. She also knew that there was another side to her husband, although out of respect she had always tended to accept it and let it lie, rather than pressing Peter about it. She knew, for example, that despite his success Peter always felt that he was underachieving. He'd make comments from time to time about how some colleague was getting this or that award or grant, and she could hear the envy, along with some resentment, in his voice. She also knew that Peter recoiled from even the slightest criticism, and that he craved support and praise, especially from her. There were times when he would pout until he got her attention.

Peter, then, was not only a sensitive man but a very insecure man. The pain and anger that he had carried inside him for all those years as a result of his experiences of betrayal at the hands of his parents turned out to be largely unconscious. By that I mean that when we first met, Peter had not yet made any connection between his youth and his present rage toward Helen. Until I pointed it out he could not see the connection between his sensitive nature, his experiences growing up, and his insecurity as an adult. He was an educated and mature man, but he still could not connect the dots that ran through his life. Once we made those connections, though, it became apparent that Peter's recent actions and emotions were driven in large part by insecurity. That insecurity had its roots in the kind of person he was, plus his experiences growing up. He had, in fact, suffered countless separations and losses—including the loss of his mother to her other relationships, and the loss of his father to illness—and these experiences had taken their toll on his sensitive disposition, causing him to become insecure.

Solving the puzzle of Peter's insecurity proved critical to saving this marriage from what surely would have been a tragic ending. For years his intense insecurity had been kept at bay, in part by his own success and in part by Helen's exceptional capacity to love. But unconsciously Peter had unrealistic expectations for relationships—for example, to never be criticized, to never experience a withdrawal of affection. On the one hand, these expectations compensated for what he perceived was lacking in his own childhood and in his parents' marriage; on the other hand, they could not reasonably be satisfied by any normal relationship.

Like Peter, Helen was a tenderhearted soul, but she was much less insecure than her husband. Peter had captured the essence of insecurity correctly when he'd said that Helen had always seemed content with herself, whereas he rarely if ever felt that way. Helen knew that Peter had not been happy growing up, but he rarely spoke about it. His father had died before they were married, and her mother-in-law had moved to another part of the country and rarely visited, which seemed to suit Peter just fine.

Helen was very sensitive to others' needs, and she possessed virtually none of Peter's mother's apparent capacity for callousness, unreliability, or exploitation. In the shelter of this loving marriage, Peter's insecurity had been pretty well contained. But then Helen's depression hit, and the changing dynamics in their relationship had aroused the demon of Peter's insecurity, which in truth had always been there, like a fault line waiting to be disturbed. Helen's depression, and the subsequent loss of the intimacy and tranquillity that Peter had enjoyed for so long, was more than enough to create the quake that unleashed his bound-up rage.

What is critical in order to help people like Peter, and relationships such as his and Helen's, is an understanding of the ways in which temperament—the dispositions we are born with—interact with our experiences to create the personality that we develop. Here we are talking about one important personality trait—insecurity—and how it can be set off in destructive ways. Only by understanding what insecurity is and where it comes from can people know what to watch out for in their own attitudes, feelings, and behavior. Peter was able to move in this direction once the pieces of the puzzle came together. He did have some insight into himself. He recognized, for example, that his reactions to Helen were out of proportion to what she had done. He even knew that he had held himself back professionally. But he did not recognize his behavior as insecurity, and that it came from his childhood. Neither did he recognize the unrealistic expectations that lay beneath his insecurity and that drove his anger and his need for reassurance.

The results of understanding insecurity, for both Peter and Helen, were positive. Within a couple of months he'd packed up his belongings and moved back home. By then Helen's depression was much improved. Equally important, they took that time to open the communication in their relationship. One thing that this led to was a clearer understanding of what had happened. They were able to take a look at the unconscious expectations that Peter had been carrying around all those years—expectations that he should never be subject to criticism, anger, or disappointment but should be loved continuously; in other words, that he could have a perfect wife. He very nearly did, which was why his massive insecurity had been able to lie relatively undisturbed for so long. For most people, insecurity rears its destructive head much sooner than that, but the reasons for it are the same: real people cannot live up to unrealistic expectations.

$$* * *$$

Insecurity, much like jealousy, is natural. Almost everyone can relate to feeling insecure (or jealous) at times. Moreover, as in Peter's case, you can't necessarily tell if someone is insecure by his or her lifestyle. The key, rather, is in how a person feels inside. A person who is very successful and who may even seem self-assured and outgoing on the surface can be quite insecure underneath. All it takes is a perceived rejection or loss to set off that insecurity. To you someone may seem to be a successful and important person, but privately he may not feel worthwhile. He may strike you as having it made, yet on the inside he may be a lot more like Peter—never at peace with or accepting of himself—than like Helen.

Since feelings of jealousy and insecurity are part of our human nature, there is no point in feeling ashamed about them. At the same time, we need to recognize that insecurity, like its cousin jealousy, has incredible destructive potential. Think about this: Simple anger, if it is not driven by insecurity or jealousy, rarely threatens to destroy us or our relationships. However, anger that is fueled by jealousy can be highly destructive to our own health and to our relationships. The same is true for anger that is driven by insecurity. I have seen both jealousy and insecurity undermine the spiritual and physical health of many individuals and destroy many relationships. It very nearly destroyed Peter's marriage.

2

The Roots of Insecurity

As important as our attachments to our parents are, these are not the only attachments we form growing up. Our experiences in relationships throughout childhood and adolescence can also contribute to whether we grow up secure or insecure. Peter, for example, would no doubt have been even more insecure if it hadn't been for his father's steadiness and reliability. True, he resented his father for not divorcing his mother, but at least his father had been there as a reliable parent for both him and his sister. Peter's marriage to Helen, plus the fact that he chose a field of work where he was talented and successful, had allowed him to carve out a niche in life where he'd been relatively insulated from criticism and conflict. Not many of us are that fortunate. If Peter had fallen in love only to be rejected, or if he'd married a coldhearted woman and been abused, or if he'd had to survive in a more competitive, dog-eat-dog work environment, I'm sure that insecurity would have colored his life more than it had.

***

Ironically, the effects of childhood separation and loss, much like the effects of physical or emotional abuse and rejection, were once thought to pass more or less quickly, leaving children with no lasting emotional scars as an individual passed from childhood to adolescence to adulthood. This misconception may be one reason why insecurity has remained so poorly understood. In reality there is no basis in fact to believe that the effects of separation and trauma on children's hearts and souls is only fleeting, or that a wounded spirit or a broken heart heals either quickly or completely.

It was once a common belief, even among experts in child development, that a young child who was separated from its mother, even for a prolonged period of time, got over the effects of that separation rather quickly. After the child was reunited with the mother following the separation, it was believed, all would soon be back to normal, emotionally and psychologically speaking. The child would bear no permanent emotional scars, and the loss would not affect him or her later on.

As popular as they were, these beliefs turn out to be false. And the same applies to the effects of abuse and neglect, both of which are experienced by children as a loss (of love). We now know that the damage does not heal quickly and that the effects appear later on.

Researchers studying children who were separated from their mothers—for example, because the mother had to go into a hospital—consistently observed that the typical first reaction of very young children to separation is to cry and protest vigorously. The great majority will be visibly agitated. Many will search up and down for their missing mothers and will continue to do so for some time. Initial efforts to comfort or nurture these young children are typically met with hostility and rejection: they don't accept the comfort, they get angry, they don't eat.

Eventually, most children can be observed to give up the hunt for mother. They stop crying (although many will still cry easily or spontaneously at times) and appear to settle down. They become quiet, almost detached; and some of the early symptoms of grief begin to fade. For example, if an adult attempts to approach a child at this point, some will still squirm away or be irritable, but less so than they did at first; many others, meanwhile, will accept the substitute nurturing in a more or less passive manner.

This state of *seeming acceptance* that children commonly move into sometime after being separated from their mothers may be what was originally mistaken for a resolution of their grief. The same observation, of course, can be made of most children who are physically or emotionally abused: at some point they settle down. In reality, though, the grief of children who lose their mothers, like the grief of those who lose love, is not resolved at all, but simply enters another stage. One source of proof for this argument is observations of what happens when young children are reunited with their mothers after a period of separation. At this point the majority will not react initially with either tears or eager affection. They will not run to their mothers with open arms. Instead, most will initially remain detached, both physically and emotionally. Many will not even look at their mothers. And if their mothers do approach them, many will actually turn away, as if giving them the cold shoulder. Only after some time has passed will most children begin to warm up to their mothers again.

This last reaction—eventually warming up—may account for why observers concluded that all was well: that the child had gotten over it, and that his or her grief had been overcome and resolved. But this is not necessarily true. Follow-up of children who had been separated from their mothers yielded results very similar to what more recent long-term studies of abused children have found. These studies showed that many of these children go on to react with intense anxiety when they are separated from their mothers again, even for a short while. A significant number of children became clingy and exceedingly anxious whenever their mothers tried to leave them. Interestingly, quite a few developed rebellious tendencies, along with shortened tempers.

The results of these long-term studies show that the effects of the initial separation—of the broken connection—did not disappear but lingered, changed form over time, and reappeared, for example, as rebelliousness, temper problems, self-abuse, or tendencies to become depressed or anxious. Finally, it was noted that these longer-term effects of broken attachments were both more frequent and more intense in males. This clearly runs counter to the popular notion that boys are born tougher and less sensitive than girls.

Although by far the most common, the above reactions are by no means the only ones that can be observed when children are separated from their mothers. There are extremes at either end, beginning with those children who appear to take any separation—even a short one—particularly hard. These children cry even harder and longer than most, and when they withdraw they appear truly forlorn, apathetic, and depressed. They stop eating, start wetting their beds at night, and show signs of acute anxiety. After they are reunited with their mothers, they soon become excessively clingy and panic at the prospect of any potential separation. Many of these children are probably among the more *interpersonally sensitive* among us, and some of them will grow up to be insecure, depending on just how much abuse, rejection, and loss they experience.

At the other end of the spectrum are those children who don't seem vulnerable at all to separation. These children don't cry or appear depressed. They don't go on a search for their missing mother for very long, if at all. Though rare, there are such children, and they are curious. Typically they are described by their parents as children who were never cuddly or affectionate, even from birth. These children, like the extremely sensitive ones, also stand out. Their mothers sometimes complain that they could not hug these children, even as infants, because they would squirm and wriggle away. They don't react with anxiety to separation; on the contrary, they tend to wander away from their mothers starting at an early age. These children are interpersonally *insensitive* by nature. Exposed to abuse and neglect, these children are at risk for becoming *emotional predators,* who as adults lack the capacity for attachment and intimacy, and who prey on sensitive people.

***

Some psychologists who observed the effects of separation on young children wondered if those effects could be avoided if the children were placed in a caring, homelike environment instead of in a residential setting, which was where the original observations had been made. The idea was that perhaps, outside of the relatively cold institutional setting, children might not react so strongly to being separated from their mothers. Two such researchers—a married couple— tried this. Over a period of several years they took into their own home a small number of children who would otherwise have been temporarily institutionalized. They went to great lengths to create a caring environment, to the extent of keeping with the parents' routine as much as possible, bringing some of the children's favorite toys as well as their own clothes with them, and visiting them in their own homes to get acquainted before the children were moved.

Researchers such as John Bowlby and others found that although in some cases they could reduce some of the worst effects of separation, they could not completely eliminate them, at least not in all children. These may well have been the more sensitive children. Sadly, the long-term effects of separation—the children's behavior after they were reunited with their parents—in most cases were virtually identical to what they were in children who'd been separated from their mothers and placed in institutions.

Observations of children separated from their mothers show that most respond to separation with behavior and emotions that could be labeled *grief*. We talked about grief earlier, and noted that there is a great deal of variability in people's response to loss. Part of that variability is due to interpersonal sensitivity and insecurity. This appears to be true for children also. A child's grief is similar to adult grief, including the fact that there are large individual differences that reflect children's differing sensitivities.

In children as well as adults, the worst of grief recedes after a while; but that does not necessarily mean that it has healed. In children, especially sensitive ones, grief typically reemerges later on; for example, when the child is reunited with the mother. It leaves residual effects, and symptoms are apt to reappear whenever the child is threatened with separation. Finally, it can have even longer-term effects. These delayed effects include behaviors ranging from withdrawal and depression, on the one hand, to aggression, self-abuse, and rebelliousness, on the other. These children grow into adolescents who have low self-esteem, who suffer from anxiety, and who are anything but comfortable with themselves. In other words, they are *insecure*. Not all children are affected equally; indeed, some children seem pretty much impervious to the effects of separation, while others are deeply affected.

It is significant that recent research on the effects of abuse and neglect have turned up symptoms in children and adolescents similar to those found in cases of abandonment or separation. It appears that what all of these experiences have in common is that they can create insecurity, especially in sensitive people. The observations of researchers, then, far from affirming any quick resolution of children's grief, reflect differences in interpersonal sensitivity and the insecurity that can eventually emerge as a result of these kinds of traumas.

***

So, what does separation mean, for example, for all those parents who have no choice but to place their infants in full-time day care, where they must endure separations from their mothers and fathers for many hours each and every day? How might this economic necessity affect those children, especially those who may have been born very interpersonally sensitive?

Similarly, what are the implications for the hundreds of thousands of children of divorce? Our divorce rate continues to be high, and the number of single-parent households and blended families continues to grow.

No matter how you look at it or justify it, divorce and reintegration into a blended family represent significant disruptions, losses, and separations for children. The symptoms of broken connections and lost attachments in our youths include alienation, depression and suicide, apathy, self-abuse, eating disorders and anxiety, rebelliousness, and youth violence. It's enough to make one wonder if, as a society, our way of life may be unintentionally leading us to raise increasing numbers of insecure children.

***

Evidence that the effects of loss do not simply disappear includes the fact that many children who experience repeated separations early on become sensitized and react very strongly to future separations. Some develop enduring behavioral problems, including tendencies to withdraw and to feel easily depressed or anxious, whereas others become rebellious, alienated, or aggressive. Reactions such as these are the prototypes for how insecure adults react to loss, rejection, and criticism. Their insecurity sensitizes these adults and leads them to perceive rejection, criticism, even abandonment when they are not really there. Others see insecure people, as Helen and I saw Peter, as *overreacting* to reality. But insecure people themselves—until they see their insecurity for what it is—see only rejection or betrayal.

* * *

Grief is perhaps the most painful of human emotions. Sensitive individuals who witness grief in others will feel that pain and experience helplessness. This can be so uncomfortable that many people are driven to avoid a grieving person altogether, to try to talk them out of their grief, or to distract them from it. Parents sometimes do this to their children. Rather than allowing them to experience and work through their grief, parents sometimes avoid dealing with it at all. Some tell their children to stop feeling sorry for themselves, while others try to distract them with some other activity. Perhaps at least some of these parents are motivated to do this because the grief of their children stirs up some painful memories of their own. Grief is the hole in your heart that gets better but never heals completely. In sensitive individuals the pain of their own grief can be restimulated through empathy with others.

HOW DID I GET TO BE INSECURE?

Besides wanting to know just how insecure they are, the next greatest concern that people express is how they got to be that way. The questionnaire below can help you understand how rejection, loss, or separation may have affected you or someone you love. To make it useful, keep in mind that your reactions to other people, here and now, are determined in part by your earlier experiences with those you were attached to as a child, combined with the kind of temperament you were born with. To understand how any insecurity in you or your partner may be affecting you today, therefore, involves assessing the experiences you each have had, and the way these affected your personality as it developed. Without this insight couples often struggle blindly with insecurity in one or both of them. Armed with this knowledge, though, individuals can do a lot to overcome their insecurity, and couples can significantly improve their relationships. As we shall see, understanding insecurity points the way to the important issues that need to be addressed in order to heal it.

The ways in which separation and loss affect us depend both on how severe they are and on when they happen. To be sure, certain losses tend to be overwhelming for the people who experience them. Children are especially vulnerable to traumatic losses and to experiences of severe abuse or neglect, all of which can create the foundation for lasting insecurity. In contrast, some people may develop insecurity not as a result of a single traumatic experience but as a result of the interaction of a sensitive nature with chronic but less dramatic experiences, such as rejection, frequent separation, indifference, or divorce. It is possible, in other words, that no one experience has to qualify as traumatic in order for a person to become insecure; rather, it may be a combination of many experiences, no one of which is obviously traumatic. This is an important point to keep in mind, since many insecure people I've talked with tend to comb their memories for traumatic incidents in the mistaken belief that their insecurity must be linked to a single event. In truth, this is rare. More typically, it is a long-standing pattern of similar experiences—such as a pattern of parental rejection or indifference over a period of many years—that is the culprit.

You can use the following questionnaire to evaluate *yourself*. Doing so will help you to understand better how insecurity might be a factor in your own personality. You can also use this material to begin to gain some insight into *someone you love* and into the dynamics of your *relationship*.

Causes-of-Insecurity Inventory

Check off each of the following that describes you (or your loved one):

_____ One of my parents was physically ill or emotionally impaired (for example, depressed) on and off for much of my youth.

_____ I spent time in foster homes or an institution when I was a child or adolescent.

_____ My family moved more than four times from the time I was born until I started high school.

_____ I have had my heart broken many times.

_____ As a child or teenager I had to leave old friends and make new ones several times.

_____ During my childhood I often had to face frightening situations alone.

_____ My mother was physically or verbally abusive to me.

_____ My father was physically or verbally abusive to me.

_____ I was often left alone as a child.

_____ I was placed in a full-time day care center before I was three years old.

_____ I was often left with baby-sitters before I started school.

_____ I had to change day care centers more than once before I started school.

_____ My mother was not an affectionate person.

_____ My father was not an affectionate person.

_____ When I was growing up my mother was often critical of me.

_____ When I was growing up my father was often critical of me.

_____ My parents fought a lot when I was a child.

_____ My parents divorced before I was ten years old.

_____ One of my parents died before I was ten years old.

_____ Both of my parents worked full-time from the time I was an infant.

_____ My mother was very impatient with me.

_____ My father was very impatient with me.

_____ Judging by the way she acted, I sometimes thought that my mother regretted having me.

_____ I was hospitalized for longer than two weeks as the result of an illness or accident before the age of six.

_____ My father showed little interest in me when I was growing up.

_____ My mother showed little interest in me when I was growing up.

_____ I missed a lot of school as a result of sickness.

_____ I had a sibling or good friend die when I was young.

_____ I was disciplined using corporal punishment.

_____ There was violence in my family when I was growing up.

_____ I was sexually abused by a family member as a child or
adolescent.

The more items that you checked off in the above list, the more
vulnerable you could be to being insecure, simply because of the
sheer number of separations and losses you've experienced. Some of
the above losses, though, such as the loss of a parent, sibling, or close
friend to death, qualify as *traumatic* losses. Many if not most people
could conceivably suffer from some degree of insecurity as the result
of even one such loss. Other losses, such as repeated separations from
those we are attached to, may not be traumatic in and of themselves,
but their cumulative effect is to create insecurity *if they occur often
enough*. As an example, consider the effect on a child of having an
impatient parent.

Impatient parents are usually unaware of just how frequently they
reject a child simply because they don't want to be bothered by them.
They may do this for any number of reasons. Some parents may be
impatient because they are depressed. Others may be distracted and
tired as a result of putting in long hours at work. Many single parents,
for example, work not one but two jobs. And still others may be too
self-absorbed or immature to pay attention to their children. In any
case, the reason for the impatience may be less important than its
effects, for when a child turns to a parent and is dismissed or ignored,
that is experienced as a *rejection*. And as anyone who's been rejected
can attest, rejection is basically experienced as a *loss of love*. Any child
who is rejected in this way on a regular basis by an impatient parent
may very well develop signs of insecurity, *especially if they are sensitive to
begin with*. This is so even though no single rejection in and of itself
could be called traumatic.

As another example, consider the accrued effects of chronic separation that is associated with placing an infant or very young child in
full-time day care. Not a few parents can relate to the tears and
tantrums that are an all too common reaction when children are
forced to separate from their primary attachments on a daily basis
long before they are ready and willing to. Caring parents may reassure

their infant child that they will see them again in six or eight hours; but the concept of time itself is something that children do not totally grasp until they are older. For a three-year-old, six hours may as well be forever. Though day care centers are hardly abusive, and although no one of these separations from a child's primary caretaker could itself be called traumatic, the cumulative effect, at least in some of the more naturally sensitive children, could be insecurity. We must always keep in mind that just because a child stops protesting after a while does not mean that the effects of repeated separations have disappeared—that they have gotten over it. It could well be that their grief has merely entered a new stage: moved underground, as grief often does, where it remains ready to reemerge in different forms at some later date.

The parent who recognizes a child's grief for what it is has an advantage over the parent who is blind to it. Their insight places this parent in a position to help a child work through grief, even if it has been buried for a long time. In contrast, the parent who does not recognize grief is more likely to react to it in ways that give a child the message that this behavior is unacceptable or inappropriate.

* * *

The insecurity that we may observe in an adult has most likely been there for a long time, and insecure behaviors in the adult have their counterparts in the child. Most of us have not taken the time to stop and think about how our behavior, or our partner's behavior, might in fact be very similar, if not identical, to ways in which we've been behaving since we were children. That's not to say that we're immature. It just means that our behavior in the present may be connected more than we realize to losses and separations we experienced long ago. In our minds we are adults, not children. We fool ourselves into believing, "That was then, this is now," as though the two were not connected. But when an adult reacts to some imagined rejection with anxiety or anger that is completely out of proportion to what is actually going on, how do we explain that? When an adult is prone to bouts of severe depression in reaction to even minor frustrations in relationships, how do we explain that? When a man or a woman reacts to even minor criticism with rage or self-abuse, how do we explain that? In each of these cases, how different, really, is the adult's behavior from that of the wounded child?

It's important to remember that a man or woman may have almost every symptom of insecurity listed earlier, yet still be perceived by others as competent and successful. Despite what a person may seem like from the outside, we don't necessarily know what's going on inside. Not a few successful people are in fact very insecure. If you observe them for a while and get to know them, though, you will eventually see that their insecurity does affect them. Their success notwithstanding, these men and women live with self-doubt and anxiety; they are uncomfortably self-conscious and prone to depression. They are not at peace with themselves. They tend to see betrayal and rejection when it isn't there, then react to it out of all proportion. Finally, they need an inordinate amount of reassurance and are extremely sensitive to criticism. As a result of these traits, all of which reflect insecurity, these men and women have trouble making relationships work.

As real and debilitating as insecurity can be, it does not mean that all is lost. If you see signs of insecurity in yourself, even severe insecurity, there is still no reason to sink into hopelessness. No matter how sensitive they are, and no matter how traumatic their past experiences may have been, insecure people are not fated to lead lives burdened by that insecurity. To start on the pathway to recovery from insecurity, the best place to begin is by understanding your present behavior and expectations, reactions and attitudes, with an eye to how these may reflect insecurity. Then, using this information and these insights as guidelines, you can create a blueprint for recovery. Part of this will involve reevaluating expectations, some of which have probably been unconscious, including your expectations for yourself and for others.

As a first step in this process, take some time to answer the following questions.

* Did you experience any losses in your childhood or adolescence that were *traumatic,* such as the divorce of your parents or the death of a parent or sibling?

* Who was the person who was your primary caretaker during your

infancy and childhood? Was your relationship with this person stable, in the sense that she or he was there every day?

* Were you separated *frequently* from your primary caretaker before the age of five? What caused these separations?

* Other than your parents, was there any other adult that you felt especially attached to as a child? If so, who was this person, and how stable was your relationship with them?

* In general, would you describe your life growing up as stable, in the sense of living in one place and growing up with the same group of friends, or not? If not, how did you react when you had to move or change friends?

* Was there someone you could reliably turn to for comfort when you were injured or upset as a child? Who was this person?

* In general, did you feel accepted and supported by your parents— or, in contrast, were one or both of them critical and rejecting of you? What were they critical of, and how often?

* Did one or both of your parents frequently use physical punishment to discipline you?

* Did you feel that your parents were interested in you as a child, or did you feel more or less ignored?

* Would you say that your parents were relatively available, or unavailable, to you when you were growing up?

If you scored high on the insecurity scale that was included in the first chapter, then the inventory at the beginning of this chapter, combined with your answers to the above questions, may give you some insights into the kinds of experiences that contributed to whatever insecurity you have. To take another step, try to recall the way you were as a child and compare it to how you sometimes might act today. For example, were you . . .

✓ prone to feeling anxious when you were alone?

✓ self-conscious (always watching yourself)?

- ✓ very self-critical?
- ✓ prone to getting angry or upset if your parents left you for any reason?
- ✓ likely to feel depressed and hopeless at times for no apparent reason?
- ✓ self-abusive at times (drinking too much, binge eating, starving yourself)?
- ✓ likely to be irritable and unhappy at times for no apparent reason?
- ✓ easily disappointed (let down) by your friends?
- ✓ worried that you weren't as talented or attractive as your peers?
- ✓ inclined to feel that people ignored you?

Do any of the above questions describe you, not only as you were when you were growing up, but as you are *now*? In other words, can you draw any *connections* between how you were as a youth and the kind of person you are today? Have any of these tendencies become issues in any relationships you've had? For example, have you had a tendency to be either depressed or angry if your partner had to leave you alone for a while, or if you felt that they were ignoring you? Have you felt easily hurt or disappointed by your partner? Have any of these issues affected you in other aspects of your life? For example, do you have any tendency to be especially self-critical? Do you experience periods of intense depression for no apparent reason? Finally, do you ever engage in self-abusive behavior, such as substance abuse or binge eating, when you are feeling either anxious or angry?

Your understanding of insecurity and how it may have affected you begins with insight into the kinds of *experiences* you've had, especially your earliest experiences with those you were attached to, and how you reacted to losses or separations, rejection or abuse. As important as experience is, though, by itself it is not usually enough to explain insecurity, especially intense insecurity. To do that, and complete the picture, you also need to appreciate the kind of *temperament* you have. That's what we'll do next.

3

The Tender Heart

ARE YOU TENDERHEARTED?

Use the questionnaire below to help you to determine if you were born with the kind of disposition that would have predisposed you to becoming insecure, if you were exposed to repeated separations from those you were attached to, or if you experienced repeated rejection or abuse. All of these things share the ability to create insecurity, because they are all experienced as a loss. Loss of what? Basically, of affection, support, and comfort. That is what attachments do for us: they provide us with a sense of worth and belonging, they help us to feel grounded, and they form the foundation of inner serenity. In contrast, broken attachments make us vulnerable to insecurity.

Again, you can apply this questionnaire to yourself or to your partner in order to gain insight into yourself and your relationship. This questionnaire measures *interpersonal sensitivity,* which is the personal disposition that lies at the core of being a tenderhearted person. Such dispositions, I believe, are largely inherited; a tendency to be interpersonally sensitive, like a tendency toward its opposite (interpersonal *in*sensitivity), is something we are born with. Both traits appear early in life and remain clearly identifiable in us throughout our lives. Individuals can usually trace a pattern of interpersonal sensitivity in their family tree. That's not to say that everyone in a family will necessarily be tenderhearted (or tough-hearted); on the other hand, a tenderhearted person can usually identify at least one person within the last generation who was like them, if they have enough information about their families. Also, interpersonal sensitivity is not a trait that is exclusive to either men or women. Some men are decidedly tenderhearted, just as some women can be described as tough-hearted.

Interpersonal Sensitivity Inventory

_____ People who know me would say that I am a very sensitive person.

_____ One of my greatest pleasures in life is to make someone else happy.

_____ It upsets me deeply if someone I like is angry at me.

_____ People described me as a sensitive child.

_____ I am an emotional person.

_____ I feel guilty if I tell even a small lie.

_____ It bothers me deeply to hurt someone else's feelings.

_____ Others would describe me as a very sympathetic person.

_____ In relationships I am quick to compromise in order to resolve a conflict.

_____ I feel passionately about many things.

_____ Having to fight with someone gets me upset, even if I know I had no choice.

_____ It has always been easy for me to understand how another person is feeling.

_____ I have a strong urge to apologize and make up after an argument.

_____ It bothers me to hear a baby cry.

_____ I feel a strong connection with nature.

_____ I go out of my way to avoid hurting even an insect.

_____ I stay in touch with friends, even those that I rarely see.

_____ I would rather keep quiet than say something that would hurt someone else's feelings.

_____ My emotions are easily moved.

_____ I get very attached to my surroundings.

_____ I can easily be moved to tears by a sad movie, television show, or newspaper story.

_____ I am a sentimental person.

_____ I will go out of my way to avoid hurting someone else's feelings.

_____ People have described me as deep.

_____ I have fallen in love many times.

_____ At work I tend to make my office or work space a home away from home.

_____ I'm the kind of person who tends to get homesick.

_____ I have a hard time cleaning house and tend to hold on to things.

_____ At heart I'm more of a stay-at-home person than an adventurer.

_____ I have taken in stray animals more than once.

_____ I have been taken advantage of at times because of my good nature.

There are many different degrees of interpersonal sensitivity and insensitivity, ranging from mild to moderate to severe. Generally speaking, extremes at either end often lead to problems, especially in relationships, where being either too sensitive or too insensitive can be a liability. For those in the middle range it is life experience that largely determines whether sensitivity or insensitivity will become a problem. Both sensitive and insensitive people are affected by loss and rejection, but in very different ways. Sensitive people can become *insecure* as a consequence of abuse, rejection, or abandonment. Insensitive people, in contrast, can become abusive and, in the extreme, even sadistic—what I call *emotional predators*—in response to those kinds of experiences.

Although it may be possible for our core dispositions, like tenderheartedness, to change, it is highly unlikely that a person could shed a disposition and replace it with another. On the other hand, it is possible to compensate for a disposition. Shy people, for example, can learn to overcome social anxiety; but shy people will tell you that although they may learn how to give a good speech, they are still shy. The same is true for interpersonal sensitivity. Trying to change your basic nature, then, would probably not prove to be worth the effort. On the other hand, it is very reasonable to look at how experience has affected your basic temperament—for example, if it's made you not just sensitive but insecure.

That brings us to an important question: if core dispositions such as interpersonal sensitivity are not easily changed, does that mean that sensitive people are doomed to become insecure, or that insecurity can never be overcome? At the other extreme, is someone whose disposition falls on the insensitive side necessarily unhealthy? Hardly.

There are many things that insecure people can do to overcome their insecurity and to recapture the sensitivity they were born with, without having to bear the added burden of insecurity. There are also things that very sensitive people can do to protect themselves. Finally, there are situations (and occupations) where relatively insensitive people thrive. Moderately insensitive persons can most definitely find fulfillment in life and in relationships, and can even successfully raise children who are innately more sensitive than they are. As we shall see, there are many situations where some tough-heartedness is not without its advantages.

***

The number of items you checked off in the above inventory will give you a rough idea of how tenderhearted you (or your partner) may be. Think about this. How do you relate to others in general? How do you behave in your intimate relationships? Has it always been easy for you, for example, to tell how others were feeling, and if so, how has this affected you? Are your moods easily affected by those of people around you? Are you emotional: easily moved to tears or laughter? Are you someone who gets attached to people, places, even things in your life?

On the other side of the coin, have you ever felt that you were taken advantage of, in your career or in love, because you don't like conflict or because your feelings were easily manipulated? Looking back on your history of relationships, do you think you may ever have gotten involved with one or more people who seemed to actually derive pleasure from fighting with you, or even from inflicting pain?

The fact that interpersonal sensitivity is not an all-or-none kind of thing means that the world is definitely *not* divided into just two groups, the sensitive versus the insensitive. There are degrees of interpersonal sensitivity. Interpersonal sensitivity, like most human dispositions, is best thought of as a *dimension* rather than as a category that you either fit into or don't. In this case the extremes of the dimension are marked by tenderheartedness at one end and tough-heartedness at the other, as in the following diagram.

Tough-Hearted <—————————————————————> Tenderhearted
                                    ^

Extremely   Somewhat   Somewhat   Extremely
   0   100

If you think of the above as a balance beam or scale, with the ^ mark denoting its fulcrum, then any one individual's disposition, in terms of interpersonal sensitivity, will be weighted toward one end or the other on the scale. The vast majority of people will fall somewhere in the middle range—between *somewhat* tough-hearted and *somewhat* tenderhearted. A much smaller number will fall at one extreme or the other: either extremely sensitive (what I call hypersensitive), or else extremely insensitive.

Having a temperament that lies at either extreme can have its liabilities. Similarly, relationships between two people whose dispositions are far apart can have difficulty. These couples often have a hard time relating to each other's fundamentally different ways of responding to the world. On the other hand, relationships between people who differ, but less dramatically, in terms of interpersonal sensitivity are common and can work very well. The deciding factor in those cases turns out to be whether the more sensitive partner is also *insecure,* and whether the less sensitive partner has any *predatory* tendencies. If either or both of these things are issues, a relationship may struggle to survive.

We'll be looking much more closely later on at the implications for relationships of differences between partners in terms of their interpersonal sensitivity. We'll see why those couples who are different from each other with respect to interpersonal sensitivity can benefit immensely from understanding how this difference plays itself out in their relationship, and how they can build an even stronger relationship based on respect for their differences.

We will also be looking at some of the issues that can arise when two tenderhearted people get together. That kind of a relationship might seem at first like a match made in heaven. In reality, however, those relationships have issues, too, though they may be different from what are typical issues in a mismatch. The issues that can come up in a relationship between two very sensitive people are best anticipated in order to avoid problems.

In preparation for this work on relationships, give both yourself and your partner a rating now, using the above scale, on interpersonal sensitivity, from 100 (extremely *tenderhearted*) to 0 (extremely *toughhearted*).

THE TENDERHEARTED PERSONALITY

In addition to the above questionnaire, the following descriptors can assist you in gaining insight into how tenderhearted you may be. As you read each descriptor, apply it to yourself and your partner.

Empathic

Tenderhearted people are highly empathic. They have sensitive emotional radar. They can read other people's feelings accurately and can also identify with those feelings. This can be a valuable asset in some circumstances; however, taken to an extreme it can be a definite liability—for example, when we hesitate to assert our own feelings or needs simply out of fear of hurting someone else's feelings. This can be a liability not only in an intimate relationship but in the workplace, and with friends and family as well.

Perhaps because of their capacity to read others' feelings and respond to them, tenderhearted people are sometimes thought of as naive or gullible, as though they believed everything they hear; but this is not necessarily true. Rather, tenderhearted people are *vulnerable*. It is true that they can be taken advantage of because they do have this exceptional capacity for empathy. If the person they are dealing with is being intentionally deceptive about their feelings—deliberately faking or exaggerating them—then a tenderhearted person can be misled and manipulated. They can be made to feel guilty, for example, by someone who exaggerates (or pretends) hurt feelings; or they may be unnecessarily intimidated by someone who exaggerates just how angry they really are. In such instances a tenderhearted person may take these supposed reactions at face value, and may try to make amends. This, of course, is what the manipulator wants in the first place. Some tenderhearted people give in a lot in relationships, or sacrifice what they want in favor of what someone else wants, simply because their partner, a friend, or a family member is good at accusing them or making them feel either anxious or guilty.

Attached

Interpersonally sensitive men and women form strong attachments to others over the course of their lives. Their ability to empathize—to experience life through the eyes of another person—forms the basis for their ability to bond with others. Sometimes called sentimental, sensitive people tend to bond not only with other people but with places and things. They get attached to their homes and their possessions. Counted in their numbers are the devoted pet owners, collectors, and conservationists among us. They make (and keep) close friends over the years, and they are especially loyal. The other side of this coin, though, is that sensitive people find it hard to break attachments to people, places, and even things.

Emotionally Transparent

Tenderhearted people wear their hearts on their sleeves. It's usually easy for others to tell how a tenderhearted person is feeling. Also, because of their heightened capacity for empathy, sensitive people often mirror what others are feeling.

Their emotional transparency can actually make interpersonally sensitive people vulnerable. They can't usually hide their feelings very well, or pretend to feel something they aren't, even if they want to. In most situations this is okay; but there are definitely times when we'd prefer to keep our feelings to ourselves, to be able to think them over without others knowing what they are.

If it's all too obvious what we're feeling, we may be vulnerable to those who read us all too easily. Tenderhearted people can be exploited, especially by people who are better able to hide their own true feelings and who are good at faking their feelings in order to gain something. Sensitive types can become the victims of emotional predators, who, quite unlike them, actually find conflict and others' pain arousing.

Idealistic

Why would tenderhearted people be idealistic? In part because they identify so easily with how others feel. Many of them become sensitized over time to injustice and unfairness. Again, this can be used against sensitive people by those who set out to deliberately exploit the tenderhearted person's sense of justice, mercy, and kindness. One man I knew gave $200 to pay for food, fuel oil, and Christmas presents for a family whose house had supposedly burned down. It turned out that this man was actually helping to pay back a compulsive gambler's bad debts.

Some of our most persistent and passionate advocates of human and animal rights and of environmental consciousness are tenderhearted people. Tenderhearted people make their moral decisions not only on the basis of what they were taught were acceptable and unacceptable *rules* of behavior while they were growing up, but also on the basis of *empathy*. Their sense of justice and injustice, or of right versus wrong, is based partly on an internal list of concrete rights and wrongs and partly on their sense of someone else's motivations and circumstances. For example, they will make a judgment about whether it is acceptable for someone to steal food not just on the basis of rules of behavior ("Thou shalt not steal") but also on a consideration of the circumstances. Using their ability to put themselves in someone else's shoes and see life through another perspective, the sensitive person may consider such factors as poverty and mental illness when deciding if stealing food is wrong. Similarly, they will base their decision on what kind of punishment is appropriate partly on an empathic understanding of the situation. In this sense tenderhearted people have an easier time understanding concepts like fairness and mercy on a gut level. In contrast, the less interpersonally sensitive a person is, the more likely it is that they will make moral decisions—for their own behavior and the behavior of others—based solely on what they learned was acceptable behavior, which turns out to have a lot to do with how a person was treated when they were growing up.

Romantic

Tenderhearted people are romantics for much the same reasons that they tend to be idealists. They can tune in to their own feelings as well as those of others, and they are perceptive with respect to the dynamics of relationships. Many of them develop an ideal of what kind of relationship two people can have together. Such ideals are important, for as we all know, if we set out goals too low we are apt to reach them! Sometimes, though, the idealism of tenderhearted people can lead to unrealistic expectations that few if any partners could meet, or else can blind them to the reality of what their partner is actually like. The former pattern is especially true of *insecure* tenderhearted people. Insecurity can cause a man or woman to focus on minor faults and failings to the exclusion of what may be essentially a very good relationship.

In other instances excessive romanticism can keep us looking at the positive, to the exclusion of some very obvious negatives that we ignore at our peril. One especially tenderhearted woman, for example, kept telling me about her husband's good side and about the potential of their relationship, even as he repeatedly abandoned and hurt her. Eventually he left her for another woman—three months after the birth of their third child. Even then, she grieved the loss of "what we could have had together." Idealism is fine, but when it distorts reality this much, the tenderhearted person can fall victim to his or her own idealism.

Emotionally Sensitive

Tenderhearted people are emotional. Their capacity for empathy allows them to identify not only with other people but, typically, with nature as well. These men and women are emotionally influenced by their environment as well as by other people. They can feel real pain, for example, by looking at pictures of rain forests being cut down.

Through this ability to identify, tenderhearted people are open to an exceptionally broad and deep range of emotional experience, from the heights of ecstasy to the pits of despair. Tenderhearted people are easily moved to tears and to laughter. Moreover, their own emotional experiences are influenced by the emotions of those around them. They know very well, for instance, that a joyful moment that is shared with someone who is happy for you and who shares your joy is very different from a joyful moment that is shared with someone who is envious of you. In contrast, interpersonally insensitive people tend to be more or less impervious to the moods of those around them; nor are they very much affected by their environment.

Many of the more intelligent of tenderhearted people among us are highly creative. However, because their feelings can also be easily hurt, it's important for the tenderhearted to learn how to identify potential predators and protect themselves from them. If they are not careful to protect their hearts, they may find them being broken time and again. And while the tenderhearted are more open to feeling, they are also more vulnerable to insecurity, to depression, and to posttraumatic stress disorders than their less sensitive counterparts.

Nonaggressive

Interpersonally sensitive people tend to prefer nonaggressive over more aggressive ways of solving problems and conflicts. This is because they empathize with others' feelings, including any pain or anxiety that another person may experience in connection with conflict. This is not to say that a secure but sensitive man or woman is necessarily conflict avoidant. On the contrary, they may be very assertive and forthright. But it's also true that they are inclined by their temperament to prefer less aggressive to more aggressive means of resolving conflicts. If driven to the point of being highly aggressive or even violent, sensitive people experience emotional distress. They definitely do *not* find aggression or violence exciting in any way. Sensing another person's fear or pain makes them upset. This is quite the opposite for interpersonally insensitive people who are subjected at an early age to abuse or abandonment. Some of these people may grow up to be adults who actually find conflict, and even violence, stimulating.

* * *

So, is it an advantage, or a disadvantage, to be a tenderhearted soul? While some may say that it's obviously better to be sensitive, the answer really depends on several factors, for instance, what area of life you're talking about and exactly *how* sensitive you are. Certainly some degree of interpersonal sensitivity is necessary for intimacy. People who lack interpersonal sensitivity definitely have a harder time understanding how another person feels. They also have a harder time than more sensitive people when it comes to identifying their own feelings. This ability to identify and share on an emotional level is the basis of emotional intimacy. Sensitive people can find it frustrating to be in a relationship with someone who is insensitive, because intimacy is harder to come by.

On the other hand, if your goal is simply to dominate and control people, rather than to relate or get close to them, then interpersonal sensitivity may be more of a liability than an asset. Are there people who really have this as a goal? I'd argue that there are, although if you are a sensitive person you may find that hard to believe. Controlling and exploiting people is easier if you remain detached and do not empathize with them. Some people say that to be successful in business these days it pays to be more tough-hearted than tenderhearted. There may well be some truth in this. After all, it must be easier to focus on the financial bottom line if you see employees as human resources rather than as living, breathing men and women with feelings, families, and aspirations. A really tough-hearted person is less likely to lose sleep over having to downsize a hundred (or a thousand) employees in order to meet corporate profit goals. I once knew an executive who was very bright and talented, and also tenderhearted. After he was forced to lay off fifty people (or lose his own job) he became so distraught that he needed intensive therapy for a year.

To be an effective *leader,* as opposed to merely a boss, requires some balance between interpersonal sensitivity and a capacity to detach. Good leaders can relate to others, but they are not so sensitive that their empathy gets in the way of being able to make decisions. They are enough in touch with their own feelings and those of others to be able to communicate effectively, which is another asset in an effective leader. Businesses do well to choose and develop managers who possess these qualities, for they are much better at building teamwork and loyalty than managers who are cool and detached.

Another factor to consider in deciding whether it's good to be tenderhearted is the *degree* to which a person is interpersonally sensitive. Although some interpersonal sensitivity may be good, there may also be truth in the adage that admonishes us that we can have too much of a good thing. Poets, writers, and artists are no doubt sensitive people. But if they are too sensitive they may not be able to withstand the criticism that one must endure in order to become successful. In its own way, extreme interpersonal sensitivity may be as dysfunctional as extreme insensitivity. Extremely tenderhearted people may be so sensitive to others' feelings that they become immobilized: phobic of conflict, and unable to bring up even minor issues that bother them for fear of hurting the other person. This leaves little room for growth in relationships and sets the stage for resentment and alienation to build up.

Finally, and perhaps most important, whether being interpersonally sensitive is an advantage or a disadvantage depends to a large extent on whether a person is also *insecure*. These two traits do not necessarily go together. Interpersonal sensitivity is a disposition we are born with; insecurity is something we learn. It is entirely possible, then, to be sensitive and also secure. However, people who are both interpersonally sensitive and insecure are, in a word, too sensitive for their own good. They tend to be defensive and very easily hurt. They can be so thin-skinned that others feel they must constantly walk on eggshells around them. They may be prone to feeling injured and to getting depressed over the smallest things. At times the things that seem to injure them deeply are a mystery to those who are in relationships with them. This reflects the fact that insecure people almost always harbor unrealistic expectations for relationships—expectations that are often unconscious—which few if any partners can live up to. This can easily strain a relationship to the breaking point.

* * *

The very best relationships I've seen are between people who are interpersonally sensitive but not to an extreme, and who are not insecure. Such relationships, needless to say, are not common. But they are useful as models. Partners in such relationships are capable of mutual empathy. Their ability to get in touch with their own feelings and to understand how the other person is feeling forms the basis not only for mutual respect but for intimacy and mutual growth. These couples are able to decide which issues are important enough to bring to a head and which ones are best let go of. And neither is so thin-skinned that it becomes necessary to walk on eggshells around each other. These qualities are goals that couples—even those who are burdened by extreme sensitivity or insecurity—can work toward.

Many people find themselves in a relationship in which neither partner's personality lies at either extreme of interpersonal sensitivity but where there is nevertheless a significant *difference* between them in interpersonal sensitivity. These mismatches may be the most challenging of all, especially if insecurity gets added to the picture. Some mismatches work out well, but many others deteriorate over time as a result of a chronic lack of communication and intimacy. We will examine these relationships, too. But first we will take a closer look at exactly how interpersonal sensitivity can lead to insecurity.

4

How Sensitivity Becomes Insecurity

Interpersonal sensitivity is an inherited disposition: if you have it, it has been with you all your life. It is different from insecurity, which can be the result of a sensitive person's exposure to abuse, neglect, or some traumatic loss. If you seem to fit the picture of being tender-hearted, see if you can identify any evidence of your being this way throughout your life. Were you, for example, considered to be a sensitive child? Were you even as a child able to sense what someone else was feeling, and to feel it yourself? Did conflict with someone else cause you distress? Did you get upset if you did something that hurt someone else's feelings? Were you moved easily to both tears and laughter?

These are only a few of the most common signs associated with being an interpersonally sensitive child. On the other end of this spectrum are those people who are born insensitive. In the extreme they were children who were never cuddly, even as infants. Typically they never showed much anxiety about being separated from their mothers; on the contrary, from an early age they were prone to wandering off. They have always had difficulty identifying with what other people are feeling and seem puzzled when something they say or do hurts someone else's feelings.

Aside from being a trait that people carry with them throughout their lives, interpersonal sensitivity is something that generally runs in families. Not that everyone in a family will be tenderhearted; however, chances are that if you are tenderhearted, you will be able to identify at least some relatives in your own generation, and perhaps some from earlier ones, who were as well.

The point has been made that it is entirely possible to be tender-hearted and secure. Basically, what is required is an accepting and nurturing environment for the sensitive person to grow up in. But as we all know only too well, not everyone is so fortunate. Abuse, neglect, loss, and rejection can turn sensitivity into insecurity. Here is an illustration of someone who was born with a tender heart and how that tender heart got turned into insecurity.

* * *

Linda was the oldest of three children in a military family, which like most such families moved around the country frequently. Linda was born in the hospital on the military base where her parents lived at the time. Her mother went into labor prematurely, two days before her father was due back from a tour of duty.

From the beginning Linda was recognized, both at home and at school, as being an exceptional and sensitive child. A quick learner, she also had a gift for fantasy and a talent for art and writing. She was an animal lover and was forever coming home with stray cats, which her mother insisted be kept outside. So Linda built a shelter out of assorted scraps of wood and other odds and ends, and fed the cats milk and scraps stolen from the refrigerator. She'd play and talk with them for hours. Eventually, each would wander off on its own, returning to the wild or perhaps to its former owner. Linda grieved these losses, but she comforted herself with fantasies about the happy life the latest cat had left her for.

Though strikingly pretty, Linda bore little physical resemblance to her parents or siblings. In addition to being artistic—a talent she also shared with no one—she turned out to be the only one of three children who didn't seem to be a born athlete. Her particular combination of temperament and traits—her looks, her sensitivity, her artistic talent, and her disinterest in competitive sports—made Linda something of a misfit in her family. She was teased relentlessly about this. Alice, her mother, often joked at family gatherings that they'd given her the wrong baby to take home from the hospital. Everyone would laugh, but Linda felt humiliated. Meanwhile, her siblings teased Linda about her lack of interest in sports, accused her of being uncoordinated, and called her Lameda instead of Linda.

Alice often remarked that if Linda reminded her of anyone, it was her own aunt Betty—Linda's great-aunt. Betty was a woman who'd had a reputation for being a spirited and unconventional soul. A talented seamstress, she'd started her own business and fared well catering to wealthy socialites, who sought her handiwork for dresses for special occasions. She'd also dabbled in painting and poetry.

After Betty died, some of her poems had been passed on to Alice for safekeeping. They were written on small pieces of paper, yellowed at the edges, and Alice had preserved them carefully between sheets of clear plastic and kept them in the back of one of her dresser drawers. One of Linda's favorite activities—starting from early childhood and continuing right through the time she left home, at age eighteen— was to ask her mother to get out Aunt Betty's poems so she could read them. When Linda was young they'd read them together, and as she grew older she liked nothing better than taking them to her room, where she could savor them in the quiet solitude. They smelled faintly of her mother's potpourri, and looked to be as old as the Dead Sea scrolls. No matter how many times she read them and no matter how glum her mood might be, the poems never failed to lift Linda's spirits.

Linda's father, Ted, was an officer who had worked his way up through the ranks, starting as an enlisted man. In the process he had elevated himself, both financially and socially, from a rough and meager Southern rural childhood to a comfortable, suburban, middle-class lifestyle.

Ted's father had been an abusive alcoholic whose financial irresponsibility, explosive personality, and unreliability at work had created a state of constant chaos and deprivation for Ted, his four siblings, and their mother. Instead of following in his father's footsteps, though, Ted had channeled his energies and set his sights on becoming anything but unreliable or irresponsible. Hence his military career. Hence his emphasis on self-discipline and his motivation for advancement.

Unlike his father, Ted drank rarely. Perhaps in reaction to the chaos he'd grown up with, he insisted that not only his own life but that of everyone in the family be governed above all else by extreme order. Unfortunately, the one quality he did seem to adopt from his father was an inclination to be impatient, explosive, and abusive at times.

Alice had also emerged from a background that was just this side of poor. For her, Ted and their marriage represented a ticket out of an existence that had seemed to her at times to be close to living death. She supported his military career completely, even though this meant living on military bases, moving every few years, and raising their children single-handedly for long stretches of time while he did any number of overseas tours of duty. She did this gladly, for she wanted a better, more stable, and more secure life every bit as much as he did.

Together Ted and Alice made their lives into a model of success that was the envy of their respective families. They ended up settling into a comfortable home in an upscale suburb of an old Southern city. By then Linda was thirteen. Ted, as a senior officer with a permanent station, no longer pulled overseas assignments or had to think about relocating the family. One might think that was a good thing, but for Linda (and to a lesser extent for her siblings, and at times, probably for Alice as well) it proved to be anything but a blessing.

As a full-time husband and father for the first time in his life, Ted asserted his presence and defined his role as more or less the commanding officer of the household. Not only was he demanding and uncompromising, but he had a short fuse and a violent temper. He could become verbally and physically abusive with very little provocation. He expected Alice to revert to being second in command from the moment he walked in the door. And he expected unquestioning, military obedience from everyone to his orders and expectations.

According to Linda, until her father came home to live permanently, her life had not been overly traumatic. I felt she underestimated, though, the cumulative effects on her sensitive nature of her family's frequent moves, plus the constant teasing she endured about her lack of athleticism and her sensitivity. She countered that the teasing tended to happen more when her father was at home, which was seldom. Still, I believed that these experiences had begun to create a measure of insecurity in Linda. For example, I pointed out that she described herself as a very self-conscious child who fretted a lot about her appearance and who worried about what her friends thought of her.

Despite the obvious disruptions caused by numerous relocations, it is nevertheless true that life on a military base is nothing if not stable and predictable, not to mention sheltered. That is what Linda meant when she said her life had not been traumatic. Never lacking for children in the neighborhood, who all shared a similar nomadic lifestyle, Linda was always able to make at least a few new friends after every move, though as she reflected on it she realized that each time it took her longer to get close to anyone.

Linda described her early years of life on military bases as quite pleasant at times. Alice, though strict, in her way was a caring mother. Every October, for example, she would make the children elaborate Halloween costumes and take them trick-or-treating on their base. And she always planned the most lovely birthday parties for them. She never worked outside the home and rarely left the children with baby-sitters. In these surroundings, and with her father away more than he was at home, Linda's innate sensitivity was somewhat protected.

All this changed abruptly when Ted came home to stay. For some reason that Linda was never able to fully comprehend, her father had always found her inherently irritating. He seemed even more impatient with her than he was with her siblings, which quickly became a major problem once Ted was home every day.

Linda had never doubted that her father found her siblings much more enjoyable company than her, and to some extent she had always understood this. For one thing, like him they were both athletic. Her younger sister was a classic tomboy, and practically from the time he could walk, her brother played virtually every sport there was. Ted was definitely and obviously drawn to them more than he was to Linda. Still, it was difficult for her to fathom the exact causes of either his apparent irritation with her or his total antipathy toward virtually all of her interests.

Starting in her freshman high school year, and not long after Ted came home to stay, Linda began to become rebellious. At the same time, she physically matured, turning seemingly overnight from a strikingly pretty girl into a tall, beautiful, and shapely young woman who drew looks wherever she went and attracted men considerably older than she. As it turned out, she was drawn to some of these somewhat older men, especially the ones who owned motorcycles.

Ted, needless to say, could not abide his teenage daughter's interest in twenty-year-old bikers. For that matter, neither could he tolerate Linda's attitudes, behavior, or girlfriends. Of course, he'd always been impatient and intolerant of her anyway. But according to Linda, now there was something more. She distinctly felt that her father not only hated her lifestyle, her choice of friends, and her interest in the opposite sex, but was uncomfortable with her sexual maturity itself. He'd never been an especially affectionate man, but she could not recall getting so much as a kiss on the cheek or a hug from him since she'd hit puberty.

Things between Linda and Ted heated up to dangerous levels during her freshman year of high school. At first their confrontations were limited to yelling, but it wasn't long before they progressed to him pushing her, then eventually hitting her. Worse, over time what was needed to provoke such reactions in Ted became less and less. It seemed that any degree of defiance at all from Linda was enough to set him off. Any failure on her part to comply, immediately, with his orders was enough to arouse his ire; and any continued resistance could trigger a violent reaction. Linda, trapped in her role as a rebellious adolescent, provided more than enough of both, and on a regular basis; and Ted reacted to it violently.

In her counseling sessions Linda recounted any number of hostile encounters with her father. There were many occasions, for example, when he would abruptly order her away from the dinner table in response to some minor comment she made, while the rest of the family sat in silence. Then there was the physical violence. Though less frequent than their verbal encounters, they hurt Linda so much more, not just physically but spiritually and emotionally. Looking back on those years, Linda said it felt like her father was trying to break her spirit, and I agreed.

Predictably, the effect of all this abuse and violence on Linda's innate sensitivity was to make her increasingly insecure. The teasing that took place during her earlier years had started this process, even if it hadn't been traumatic. But in the face of her father's intolerance, his rejection of her, and his physical abusiveness, her self-esteem, her basic sense of worth, and her sense of her place and value in the world were steadily eroded.

As an adult Linda had two major resentments. As you might imagine, she resented her father. She resented his rigidity, his rejection of her, and his abuse. But she also harbored resentment toward her mother for not intervening to protect her. Her more favored siblings were by and large spared at least the physical abuse she'd suffered. Beyond that, they were more successful than Linda ever was at building some kind of connection to Ted, based in part on athletics. Her sister, for example, won a collegiate athletic scholarship. Her brother, meanwhile, though he seemed to have inherited his grandfather's taste for liquor, nevertheless went on to a successful career in law. He was also an avid baseball fan and the holder of two seasons tickets that he frequently shared with his father.

Not surprisingly, adult relationships for Linda had been a problem. She left home at age eighteen, very soon after graduating from high school. Shortly thereafter she moved to another state with her boyfriend, Don, who had just graduated college. Six months later she was pregnant, and three months after that she and Don were married. He refused to buy her an engagement ring. Her parents, meanwhile, turned down her wedding invitation, though after her son was born Linda's mother called, then sent a gift along with a note inviting them to visit. It turned out, Linda later discovered, that Ted had forbidden Alice from having any contact with Linda, and that Alice did so only when she finally could stand it no longer and rebelled. By the time a visit could be arranged, though, Linda's son was already over a year old.

Though Don proved to be less violent than Linda's father, he was no less harsh or intolerant. He expected Linda to keep the house, raise their son, cook meals, have regular sex with him, and nothing else. He kept her on a strict budget and fought with her whenever she wanted to buy clothes for herself. In virtually every area she could think of, Don was constantly critical of Linda. For ten years, Linda said, she and Don never once went out to a restaurant, and only twice that she could recall did they go to a movie.

Linda found that Don, much like her father, was not much interested in what interested her. He didn't like to read, hated the idea of pets, and much preferred watching television to talking. She was not able to get much emotional support from him, and she found that for him, physical affection was limited to sex. It wasn't long before communication between them had dwindled to a trickle.

Don was clearly insensitive and hostile, but despite this, as well as his stinginess—financially and emotionally—Linda opted to stay with him. In fact, for a long time she felt dependent on Don, so much so that when he would threaten her with divorce—which he did regularly, whenever he was angry or displeased with her—Linda would panic.

When their son turned six, Linda told Don that she wanted to get a part-time job and use the money she earned to pay for college courses. Don resisted both ideas. Her place was at home, he said flatly. In her first independent act since marrying Don, Linda went ahead and did it anyway. She was dying for intellectual stimulation, she told me, and also for contact with people she could talk to. As much as a means to get an education, Linda saw college as a way to make new friends and break free from the isolation of her life.

For the next two years Linda's relationship with Don deteriorated even more, to the point where it became, in her words, a living hell. They fought all the time. Don would not let go of his resentment at Linda for opposing him, nor would he relent and support her decision to go to college, even when she proved to be an exemplary student. He made it known that he was not interested in hearing anything about her classes. At the same time his criticisms of her housekeeping and parenting increased. Except for increasingly rare occasions when Linda would give in to Don's complaints, sex between them ended. Linda threw herself into parenting and studying as ways of minimizing her day-to-day contact with Don. As much as she could manage they'd spend their evenings in different rooms.

In spite of the tension at home, Linda said that she felt happier during this time than she had in years. She thoroughly enjoyed both motherhood and school, and as she had hoped, she did make some new friends. All in all, she said, she felt more alive, both emotionally and intellectually, than she had since childhood. In these ways you could say that Linda's self-esteem was on the rise at this point in her life. Her experiences at school nurtured her sensitivity in ways that neither her family nor her marriage ever had. However, she was still extremely *insecure*. She remained self-conscious and self-critical, was easily hurt, was prone to anxiety, and felt unsure about what people thought of her. That was the enduring legacy of her abusive relationship with her father.

At the start of her third year of school Linda met a man in one of her classes. "He expressed an interest in me," she said, flashing a bright smile, "and that was enough." Also, he was good looking, and he shared her interest in creative writing. And last but not least, she added with a giggle, he had a motorcycle. They started meeting for coffee after class, and it wasn't long before they began an affair.

After six months or so, Don caught on. His discovery of Linda's affair led to the inevitable shouts and self-righteous accusations that are typical of people, like Don, who create their own self-fulfilling prophecy only to staunchly refuse to acknowledge the role they play in it. They all but drive their partners to look elsewhere for affection, support, and stimulation, and then feel betrayed when their partners do just that.

About a month after finding out about Linda's affair, Don moved out and filed for a divorce. Once again she was free—of unreasonable control, of constant disapproval and rejection, and of abuse. However, in her subsequent relationships, including two long-term live-in relationships, Linda was not able to find happiness any more than she had with Don—not able to find the support, affection, or sense of human connectedness that she'd craved since childhood. A pattern kept repeating itself in that she seemed drawn, like a moth to a flame, to men who were very much like her father and Don: demanding, critical, and ultimately rejecting. No matter how well they started out, her relationships inevitably became poisoned by chronic conflict. She always seemed to displease the man she was with, and she in turn was always feeling let down and abused.

That was Linda's situation when she started therapy. When I first met her she had completed her undergraduate education, was working for a large firm as a graphic artist, and was taking evening courses in business administration, in which she was once again academically very successful. She was a tall and slender woman, with dark red hair, fair skin, and deep brown eyes. Her voice bore just a trace of a Southern accent. It was easy to see why men had always been attracted to her. In spite of her physical and intellectual assets, though, Linda was a good example of a very insecure person.

What were some of Linda's symptoms of insecurity? The list was long. For one thing, despite the fact that she got A's in almost all of her courses and was highly regarded by her teachers for her ability to think critically and creatively, Linda expressed constant anxieties about her course work. Her expectations for herself were not just high but unrealistically high, to the point where even the slightest criticism would trigger depression and feelings of self-hatred. No matter how successful she might be, in her eyes she was always screwing up. She was extremely self-conscious and fretted incessantly about her appearance, feeling that her hair was too straight, her complexion too sensitive, her legs too skinny, and so on.

Linda also worried that she came across to others as an airhead. That turned out to be a leftover from childhood, too, for in her family the general attitude toward artistic people was that they were flaky. Linda was eternally vigilant for criticism and rejection by others, often perceiving one or the other when, from the stories she told, it wasn't clear to me that either was intended.

I learned from Linda that she had sometimes been accused of being falsely modest, and also of being aloof and unfriendly. When I asked her to talk to her best friends about this, just to check it out, she came back and reported that her friends had said that some people they knew found it hard to believe that Linda was truly so insecure. She was, after all, both bright and beautiful. What these people were doing, I suggested, was mistaking Linda's shyness for conceit, and her anxiety for vanity. Being as insecure as she was, Linda was giving off signals that others misinterpreted. They felt that she was putting them off; meanwhile, she was feeling self-conscious and worried about being rejected by them. What a vicious cycle!

Another symptom of insecurity in Linda was her jealousy of her friends' relationships with one another. Though it had never actually happened, she constantly feared that her friends would abandon her: that they would abruptly decide for some reason either that they just didn't like her anymore, or else that they liked someone else better, and in either case drop her. She worried that people talked about her behind her back, finding fault, or that some women who she thought disliked her were trying to turn others against her.

For a long time Linda tried to convince me that she never met any men who were not like Don or her father, but eventually she came to see that she met many men, but in part it was she who was *choosing* such men to get involved with. For some reason she could not understand, men who her friends liked were not attractive to Linda; on the other hand, the men she did get involved with were usually disliked by her friends, and vice versa. She was not very good at judging men's character. Instead of taking the time to get to know them well and look beyond first impressions, she tended to choose men who talked a good game and came on as self-assured, which was much the way her father presented himself.

On an even deeper level, Linda could not understand why I thought she held unrealistic expectations for how an intimate relationship should be. That was not unusual, though, since like many insecure people she had never really taken the time to put her expectations into words, or think about them consciously. As we talked more about relationships, though, she revealed some ideas that, for me, clearly translated into unrealistic expectations. She found it hard to understand, for example, why a man who *truly* loved a woman could ever do anything to hurt her. And she thought it was reasonable that a *really* happy couple would never have to fight. She admitted that these ideas might be idealistic, but she didn't see them as unrealistic. I suggested that they were not just idealistic but unrealistic. Even loving men, I said, sometimes hurt the women they loved; and even the happiest couples had occasion to argue. That was not to say that she should expect abuse or chronic conflict. On the other hand, expecting just the opposite was, I said, inviting certain disappointment.

Her unrealistic expectations contributed to the dysfunction and frustration that Linda experienced in her relationships. To say she was thin-skinned was putting it mildly. She was eternally vigilant for any little thing that someone—friend or partner—might say or do that could possibly be construed as critical or rejecting. It was not only outright and intentional criticism, though, that would upset Linda; even the slightest comment could be perceived as criticism, hurt her feelings, and elicit a defensive reaction. Many of the supposed slights she talked to me about struck me as unintentional rather than deliberate. For a long time she had a very hard time seeing that as a possibility. Moreover, her actions in relationships were guided by these expectations, with disastrous results.

I came to see how at least some men, sensing Linda's insecurity, could use it against her. They could do this by using the same strategy that Don had for years, which was to find fault with Linda and put her on the defensive. Invariably, she would react by worrying obsessively. She would try to make up for whatever shortcoming she felt she was being accused of. Her anxiety would drive her to talk incessantly about whatever the supposed fault was. According to her, this would only end up irritating her partner all the more. She'd often been accused of talking things to death.

Linda sought constant reassurance from whatever man was in her life: reassurance that he liked her, that she was attractive, and that their relationship was okay. She was ever vigilant for any glance that might be cast in the direction of another woman. She would feel hurt if she dressed up and failed to get a compliment, or even if the compliment seemed lukewarm. Not only did these tendencies make her vulnerabilities transparent to others, but like her tendency to talk issues to death, they could be irritating to others. She told me that the most common complaints she got from boyfriends, aside from their feeling that she talked things to death, were that she was too sensitive, wanted too much attention, and was vain.

After a while every one of Linda's relationships became more and more conflictual. As many times as this pattern repeated itself, though, she remained blind to the role that she played in creating it, in terms of both the men she was drawn to and the dynamics she helped to establish in these relationships through her expectations. The conflict in her relationships usually escalated so that from Linda's point of view, she was being abused, whereas from her partner's point of view, she was being demanding and bitchy. At that stage the end was usually not far off.

* * *

Linda is not only a good illustration of an insecure person—and of how insecurity undermines relationships—but also a good example of how interpersonal sensitivity can lead to insecurity. Linda was—and always had been—a tenderhearted person by nature. Whenever we experience the loss of love, support, and nurturing from those to whom we are attached, the effect is to create insecurity. This effect is all the greater for those, like Linda, who have interpersonally sensitive dispositions. Her descriptions of herself as a child made it apparent that Linda had the characteristics of an interpersonally sensitive person. From the start she was rather different from her parents and from her siblings. If she was like anyone in her family it was her great-aunt Betty. Linda appeared to have inherited this woman's temperament. Even as a young child she had a reputation in the family for being sensitive and thin-skinned—an artsy type—in clear contrast to her sister's tomboy personality and her brother's jock personality. While they pursued sports and loved rough-and-tumble play, Linda constructed elaborate fantasy games, painted, played dress-up, and labored over her first poems. By the time Linda graduated high school, she'd already had several poems published in local newspapers, as well as in her high school yearbook.

While her sensitivity had made her vulnerable, the root causes of Linda's insecurity lay first in the teasing and ridicule she'd endured as a child. Though her tormentors may have tried to pass it off as harmless fun, such teasing is experienced as painful and abusive when you're on the receiving end. The fact that she was different was turned into a sense of inferiority that Linda carried with her right into adulthood.

Then there was the abuse and rejection by Linda's father, and also in what she perceived to be her abandonment by her mother, who from Linda's point of view had stood by and condoned her abuse. These experiences of rejection, betrayal, and loss of love and affection were repeated not only in Linda's marriage to Don but in her other relationships as well. Regardless of whether Linda played a role in this process—for example, by choosing an insensitive, abusive husband—the fact was that, psychologically and emotionally, she continued to experience losses, abuse, and rejection.

* * *

Interpersonal sensitivity, much like other dispositions we are born with and that together make up our temperament, is something that is not likely to change much over time. On the other hand, the effects that experience can have on our disposition, such as the insecurity that comes from abuse, loss, or rejection, *can* be changed. No matter how insecure you may believe you are, you must always keep this in mind: while sensitivity is something we are born with, insecurity comes from experience. It is basically something that we *learn*.

In order to conquer insecurity, the change process must begin with *awareness*. Unfortunately, most people who are insecure do not perceive it or understand it well. Therefore, they are at a loss for how to change it. That was certainly true for Linda, who felt confused and hopeless at the outset of therapy. In order to help her and people like her, the starting point is to clear up their confusion about how they got into their situations. Linda needed to appreciate that *both* the kinds of experiences she'd had *and* the nature of her personality and temperament had played important roles in creating her insecurity.

While Linda probably could not change her basic temperament, understanding her insecurity, and what had caused it, and the role it played in her relationships opened the way for her to change. In time she was able to learn to identify (and avoid) the wrong men, to change her expectations for relationships, and to work on reducing her insecurity. This process is not unlike understanding that you have a family history of breast cancer or depression: you can't change your genes, but knowing what you are vulnerable enables you to manage and anticipate your feelings. That kind of insight can allow you at the very least to reduce your risk, and possibly even avoid problems. This is as true for insecurity as it is for depression or cancer.

Healing begins with the above insights, plus understanding that there is nothing wrong or abnormal about being tenderhearted. People vary in how interpersonally sensitive they are. Being extremely sensitive may make someone more vulnerable to insecurity, but in itself it is in no way a sign of pathology. Moreover, there's nothing a sensitive person can do about being sensitive. However, many sensitive individuals have reported to me that they were teased, even ridiculed, all their lives for being the way they are. "Don't be so sensitive!" is the admonishment these people often get, as Linda did, from family, teachers, sometimes even friends. This kind of advice is not helpful. It usually leads to nothing but frustration and shame.

**

If you are tenderhearted, not pathologizing yourself for being that way can be an important first step toward relieving any feelings of shame you may have about being the way you are, or frustration over being unable to change. Such feelings will only serve to complicate any insecurity you may already have. One man told me that for as long as he could remember he'd been ashamed of being sensitive. "It definitely was not considered manly in my family," John said. Like Linda's, his temperament was much more similar to an ancestor's than it was to that of anyone in either his own or his parents' generation. For years John tried to make himself tougher. As a teen he got involved in competitive physical sports. He built up his body. He hung out with guys who had a reputation for being tough. He even took up boxing. Yet his passion was always for writing, and in his relationships he had little appetite for fighting, or even arguing. He went on to have two unsuccessful marriages to women who were aggressive and much less sensitive than he. They ended up treating him with disdain and abusing him.

For John and Linda, understanding that they were highly sensitive, and had been born that way, and (most important) that they would be much better off accepting this and taking it into account than fighting it marked a turning point in their lives.

**

Insecurity can lurk beneath the surface in a personality that otherwise seems quite healthy and robust. For example, on first impression Linda appeared much different than she really was. Many people found it hard to believe, based on limited knowledge of her, that she was truly insecure; instead, they interpreted her behavior as vanity or snobbishness. People tend to judge others on the basis of certain qualities, especially their appearance, their intelligence, and the kind of work they do. On all of these measures Linda scored high. Her self-esteem, which had been quite low for many years, had actually increased over the years as a result of her successes as a mother and as a student. Despite all this, she remained very insecure, and also blind to the role that insecurity was playing in undermining her relationships. Her insecurity became obvious, though, once you got to know what was going on *inside* Linda.

While self-esteem in many ways is based in our abilities and our personal assets, the roots of insecurity run deeper. However tempting it may be to assume that personal success precludes insecurity, that clearly is not necessarily so. On the contrary, many talented and successful men and women are surprisingly insecure. John was a good example of this. As a child he was teased and ridiculed for being too sensitive, not competitive enough, and soft. In high school he tried to hide his sensitivity and compensate for the nagging feeling that he was not man enough through competitive sports and bodybuilding. Academically he excelled, winning a scholarship to an Ivy League college. As an adult he was a successful real estate developer. Yet he was still insecure. Because of his sensitivity he'd never thought of himself as being man enough, and the constant ridicule from his family had left him with many symptoms of insecurity.

Soon we'll be taking a closer look at what an insecure man or woman can do to try to shed insecurity without sacrificing sensitivity, and also how insecurity shows up in men versus women. There is much that an insecure person can do to recapture their innate sensitivity. The road back—from insecurity to sensitivity—begins with the kind of awareness that has been the focus of these first four chapters. Before moving on, then, it can be helpful to spend some time reflecting on this material. To what extent does the theory of sensitivity and insecurity presented here apply to you or to someone you love? Do you know anyone—including yourself—who may in fact feel proud of themselves in many ways, yet also be very insecure? Can you trace that insecurity, from its origins in interpersonal sensitivity to its being the eventual result of loss, rejection, or abuse? If so, then this understanding will be the starting point for eventual recovery from insecurity.

5

Tough-Hearted People

Sensitivity is part of our temperament. People are born with a degree of sensitivity that they carry with them throughout their lives. Insecurity is the result of subjecting an innately sensitive person to abuse, rejection, or traumatic loss. The age at which these things happen, as well as how severe they are and how long they go on, is what determines how insecure a sensitive person will become.

But what about the other side of the coin? Are there people whose natural temperament could be called insensitive; and if so, what do we know about those people? Also, if traumatic losses or abuse make the sensitive person insecure, then what happens if an insensitive person has such experiences?

Interpersonal sensitivity is part of the temperament we are born with. It follows, then, that insensitive people have also been that way all their lives. Most people, of course, whether they are sensitive or insensitive, do not fall at one or the other extreme; rather, their temperaments fall somewhere in the middle range, somewhere between *moderately* sensitive and *moderately* insensitive. For one thing, this means that couples who are somewhat different in terms of sensitivity can still make their relationships work; for another, it means that people who differ in terms of sensitivity can still work effectively as teams and get things done in their communities and in the workplace.

In contrast, being born with a temperament that lies at one *extreme* or another—either hypersensitive or extremely insensitive—may be more of a liability than an asset. Although one might think that being sensitive is a desirable quality to have, some people are so interpersonally sensitive that it handicaps them more than it helps them. They may, for example, become phobic of conflict. This can happen when a hypersensitive person consistently hesitates to assert themselves because doing so might hurt (or just inconvenience) someone else. They become so hesitant to cause even a little discomfort in others that they fail to get their own needs met. One emotional consequence of this is that they live in a state of chronic depression; another is that they can build up stores of resentment that lead in the end to destructive self-pity.

Perhaps the worst aspect of being hypersensitive, though, is that it makes a person exceptionally vulnerable to being manipulated by others. Highly sensitive people are easy to read, and they empathize easily with others. Highly sensitive people can find that their ability to empathize can be used against them, such as when someone plays on their sympathy, or manipulates them into feeling guilty.

The fact that sensitive people are more likely to become insecure when subjected to serious losses or abuse is another reason to view interpersonal sensitivity, especially in its more extreme forms, as not just a blessing but a blessing that needs to be protected.

There are some arenas in life where it may pay to be either not too interpersonally sensitive or even somewhat insensitive. The contemporary corporate world and perhaps even the contemporary American family may be two of these.

The second half of the twentieth century has witnessed several social trends that, together, have transformed family life and the American workplace. First, we have become a mobile society. Today's children must expect to move a number of times during their parents' productive years. This has meant that they must adjust to leading lives of broken connections as they separate repeatedly from friends and homes, as well as lives of relative isolation from their extended families. It has meant that the sense of community and stability that comes from living for many years in the same house, in the same neighborhood, with the same friends, and having regular contact with grandparents, uncles and aunts, and cousins, is a rare experience for children today. Even moving to a nicer neighborhood and a bigger house may have its psychological downside, particularly for very sensitive children.

The second trend has been the emergence of dual-career and single-parent families as the norm. Fewer and fewer people can even remember days when family life was based on complementarity: where one parent was responsible for some aspects of daily life and the other was responsible for others. The most obvious example of this is the now nearly extinct single-breadwinner family. Everyone, it seems, is working these days, with many parents holding down both a full-time and a part-time job in order to make ends meet. As a coworker and father of an infant daughter once said to me, "I'm working five days and four nights a week, and there still doesn't seem to be enough money to pay the bills." I knew this man well, and he was far from extravagant when it came to his lifestyle. However, in order for his wife to be able to stay home and be a full-time mother, this was how hard he had to work.

It has been well documented that adults today work longer hours than previous generations; consequently our children and teenagers spend more time without parental supervision than previous generations. More and more children are placed in full-time day care before the age of three, and countless numbers are "latchkey children," who return to an empty home each day after school. Again, highly sensitive children may feel the negative effects of the relative absence of parents that is the unavoidable consequence of our changing society.

The third major change that has come to define our contemporary social environment has been the decline of what I call the "parent company." This refers to an unwritten contract between an employer and its employees in which the company's practices communicate a particular message: that it will reward hard work and commitment from its employees with a lifelong commitment in return. This kind of employee-employer contract was once common, but over the past twenty years it has declined steadily. Few people I speak to today feel that they have anything remotely like that kind of contract with their employer. On the contrary, the commitment, from both sides, tends to be pretty thin and fragile.

Considering the above, you could argue that sensitivity may be more of a liability than an asset in the both the contemporary home and the contemporary corporate environment. In neither place does it pay to be a person who forms strong attachments, for example, because chances are you will not enjoy the luxury of long-term relationships with your friends or your coworkers. As a child you will have less daily contact with your parents than they did with their parents; meanwhile, your extended family may be little more than an abstract concept. And it is foolish today for employees to commit to the company, since the company is not committed to them. Similarly, it might be equally foolish to invest a lot in, and form an attachment to, a community in which you can expect to live for only a few years.

In coping with modern life, one could argue that being at least slightly insensitive may not be such a bad thing after all. Clearly, being the opposite, especially being a very tenderhearted person, could lead to a lot of pain, and possibly to insecurity.

THE TOUGH-HEARTED PERSONALITY

It's important to remember that people vary in how insensitive they may be, just as people vary in how sensitive they are. That said, what follows is a description of the person whose natural temperament leans toward interpersonal insensitivity, or what I call *tough-heartedness.*

Nonempathic

If the essence of interpersonal sensitivity lies in a person's capacity to empathize, then it follows that people whose natural temperament falls on the opposite side of this dimension are less able to do this. The term *insensitive,* however, might leave the impression that these are people who have no emotions, but this is not true. For that reason I prefer to call these people *tough-hearted.*

Tough-hearted people have feelings and needs, just as tenderhearted people do. However they are less *interpersonally* sensitive; they are less in tune with what *other people* are feeling. Naturally, their own emotional experiences are therefore also less influenced by what others around them are feeling.

Detached

Sensitive people are prone to becoming attached: to people, places, and even things. This is much less true for those who are tough-hearted. One consequence of this is that tough-hearted men and women, and boys and girls, have an easier time with change, and in particular with separating from people, places, and things. These are men and women who do not invest themselves to any great extent in their surroundings or their possessions or, sometimes, their relationships. At work they don't make their office into a home away from home. Similarly, although they may acquire things and be as materialistic as the next person, they don't develop as much of an attachment to them. They may have friends, but they don't miss them a great deal if they have to leave them; and they don't put as much effort into maintaining relationships as tenderhearted people typically do.

Emotionally Opaque

If sensitive people could be said to be emotionally *transparent,* then interpersonally insensitive people could be said to be emotionally *opaque.* Sometimes they're described by others as *inscrutable.* If you ask them what they're feeling, tough-hearted people are as apt to shrug as to give you an answer. It's not that they don't have feelings, because they most certainly do. Generally, though, interpersonally insensitive people spend less time monitoring their own emotional state than their more sensitive counterparts do. They may need to stop and think about it before they can tell you what they're feeling. In addition, while sensitive people find their emotions are stirred often and easily in response to others, this is less true for those who are tough-hearted. These two qualities, in turn, may be connected: it could be that having their emotions stirred easily leads the tenderhearted person to develop more awareness of them, whereas being less emotionally responsive allows tough-hearted people to focus on other things. Having more experience with their own emotions may also lead the tenderhearted to being better at putting what they feel into words, and in drawing fine discriminations, as for example knowing the difference between feeling just *happy,* versus *joyful, ecstatic,* or *pleased.*

Again, it is not that insensitive people lack feeling; rather, their dispositions are such that their emotional lives are not as rich as those of sensitive people, and their emotional lives are more insulated from what others are feeling.

Hardheaded

Tough-hearted people are best described as pragmatic, or *hardheaded,* in contrast to tenderhearted types, who tend to be more idealistic and romantic. They are less moved, on an emotional level, by romantic or idealistic notions than are tenderhearted people. Morally, tough-hearted people are more inclined to make decisions and cast judgments on an intellectual basis than on an emotional one. In other words, they rely more on rules, less on circumstances, to determine if a behavior is right. It is important to understand, though, that the rules that govern the tough-hearted person's ideas come only partly from what they are *told* when they are growing up. A much more important influence on their morality is what they *observe* growing up (how the significant people in their lives behave), as well as how they themselves are *treated* by the significant adults in their lives. If they observe fairness and honesty, for example, and are treated that way themselves, then those are the yardsticks they will use in turn to judge others by. But if they observe something different, or are treated in ways that contradict what they are told, then this will influence their ideas of what is acceptable versus unacceptable behavior.

***

Let's take a look at two women, one tenderhearted, the other more tough-hearted. These two women have known each other ever since meeting as freshmen in college. Both went on to graduate school and from there to business management careers. Now in their early thirties, they remain friends. But the differences in their temperaments are reflected in dramatic differences in their lifestyles.

Jennifer, the tenderhearted one, leads a life filled with attachments. Her home, though well maintained and clean, is nevertheless crammed with furniture, photos, artwork, two cats, and all sorts of possessions. A pile of unframed photos nearly spills over on a table beside her living room couch. Walking into her home, one immediately has a feeling of warmth. At work, her office, though organized, is nevertheless filled with memorabilia and photos: her cats, her family, her boyfriend.

Jennifer has strong attachments to her friends, including Jessica. She stays in touch with them, sees them regularly, and is often the one to initiate contact. If she knows they are ill, or just having a hard time, she calls them more often than usual, or sends them a card. She is aware that she is usually the one who has to initiate contact with Jessica, and sometimes she wishes that Jessica would take the initiative. But she is also aware that they are different people; moreover, she believes that Jessica really cares for her, despite what she sees as Jessica's aloofness.

Being as attached as she is to things, Jennifer doesn't like change very much. She found it difficult, for example, when she had to change offices, which she had to do when she recently got a promotion. She liked the promotion, but she would just as soon have kept the old office. She tends to hold on to things, too, with the result that her basement is filled with odds and ends she knows she'll probably never use again but can't bring herself to part with. She likes wearing flowered dresses, and she owns a vast and growing collection of antique jewelry.

In contrast to Jennifer, Jessica's lifestyle is spartan. She owns a condo, which is comfortable but sparsely decorated. She has no pets. Her office at work is even less personalized than her home. Her preferred style of dress is similar to the way she decorates her home. She dislikes frills, prefers solid colors to patterns, and as far as jewelry goes she rarely wears anything more than simple post earrings and thin necklaces. She wears a lot of black, with red accents, which she feels (correctly) go well with her blond hair and brown eyes. Both her office and her home convey a feeling of order, if not coolness. She detests clutter, and makes a point of cleaning house at least once a year, throwing many things out. The only evidence of her broader life, in her home, are some family photos. These stand, framed in bright chrome frames, on a shelf on a built-in bookcase in her living room.

Other than that there are a couple of books on bicycling—her favorite form of exercise—on a coffee table in the living room, plus a few travel books on some of the places she's considering for her next vacation. Her office at work contains only a few personal photos, and none of the mementos and souvenirs that fill Jennifer's walls and line her bookcases.

Unlike her friend Jennifer, Jessica feels relatively comfortable with change, especially if that change happens to be a promotion. Aside from Jennifer she has a small circle of friends, but she rarely speaks with any one of them more than once a week.

＊

Jennifer is also a very romantic person. She's been seeing her boyfriend, Rick, for two years. Recently he brought up the idea of living together. Jennifer feels that she'd rather wait a while longer, to see if Rick feels strongly enough about their relationship to talk about marriage. He earns roughly half of what she does, and she knows that this will probably always be so; but he's reliable and hardworking, and has a lot of practical skills.

Jessica teases Jennifer sometimes about the fact that Rick makes so much less money than she does. Though she respects her friend's commitment, Jessica's approach to looking for relationships is much more practical. "I can tell if a man is a good prospect by the shoes he's wearing," she says. And she isn't kidding. Whenever they go out together Jessica scopes out the scene for single men. She won't even bother exchanging a glance with a man unless he strikes her as having the clothes to suggest he's got some money. In her mind, she could never feel right committing to a man who was less successful than she, and her biggest worry is that a man might look to her to support him.

Jennifer is known to her friends for having a soft heart. She's the kind of person who volunteers often to collect for charities in the office; and she sponsors a "foster child" in a third-world country. She's also the kind of person who forms strong attachments and who identifies with others' feelings. When several people in her office lost their jobs in a corporate downsizing the year before, she found herself feeling sad for a week afterward. She felt sad partly because she knew she would miss them; but mostly she felt bad because she knew that many of them had young children, one was a single mother, and another had two children in college.

Jessica also had experiences with downsizing, once when her company's projected profits did not meet expectations and another time after it decided to outsource some of its operations. Each time she, like Jennifer, was concerned; but unlike Jennifer, Jessica was less concerned about others and much more about herself: about whether she, too, might become a victim of either downsizing or outsourcing.

***

Here we have two friends, neither of whom, I'd argue, could be called dysfunctional or pathological in any way. Nevertheless, they have distinctly different personalities and lead different lifestyles, based on their different temperaments, and specifically on differences between them in interpersonal sensitivity. Neither Jennifer nor Jessica has ever been exposed to any unusual traumas or losses. They were never abused or abandoned. Both come from intact families. Their respective parents are still married after forty-plus years. Finally, Jennifer has few if any symptoms of insecurity; and for her part, Jessica has none of the problems—to be discussed later—associated with tough-hearted people who are abused as children.

It is also easy to imagine how both of these women, *with the wrong partners,* could end up being very unhappy. Jennifer, for example, clearly needs someone who would be comfortable with her sensitivity and lifestyle. We can easily imagine, too, how certain work environments might not be ones that she would thrive in. Already, Jennifer is experiencing some discomfort in a job where she must adapt to frequent changes. In counseling she's been discussing options, including going back to school for further training. Her goal is to find a job that will be more stable, even if that means that there is less upward mobility. With respect to friendships, Jennifer is best off being aware of her own sensitivity and the differences between her disposition and that of others. If she finds herself being hurt, say, by Jessica's insensitivity, then she is much better off either backing off somewhat in that relationship or else seeking out friends who are more like her. One thing she definitely should *not* do is try to change Jessica's personality. That will only lead to frustration and disappointment, and quite possibly to being rejected by Jessica. There is a false assumption that tenderhearted people are vulnerable to making, which is that others are really like them: that you can uncover the tenderness in a fundamentally insensitive person. This has led to nothing but disappointment and misery for countless tenderhearted souls.

* * *

If extreme sensitivity can be a problem, then what about those people whose temperaments place them at the other extreme—people who are very interpersonally *in*sensitive? These people have temperaments similar to Jessica's, only more extreme. In relationships and in the workplace, their temperaments can be a handicap. They are in touch with what *they* want, and to some extent they know what *they* are feeling; but they have a much harder time understanding how *another person* is feeling. They aren't mean, so much as they are blind in this area. This makes them poor leaders, since effective leadership and team building requires some capacity to empathize—to connect with others. As supervisors, very tough-hearted people can *drive* others, through intimidation for example; but they have a difficult time *motivating* others. Perhaps you have worked for someone who operated this way. If so, you know that they can get people to do things, through rewards or punishments; but they are not so successful at creating loyalty or at building teamwork.

Because of their deficit in empathy, it is all but impossible for *extremely* tough-hearted people to be intimate. Intimacy depends on the ability to articulate one's own emotional experience, and also on the ability to empathize with another person's emotional experience. The very tough-hearted just can't do either one of these things very well. So others find it very difficult to connect with them.

It takes a long time indeed for the truly tough-hearted person to form any significant attachments, if they can do so at all. At times their extreme detachment can make them appear cruel and callous. However, I have learned that unless they've been the victims of severe abuse, tough-hearted people are not *intentionally* cruel or callous, and they act surprised when someone accuses them of being so. They do, however, show little reaction to the loss of a relationship, except in so far as it may have been the source of some gratification for them that is now lost. Again, this can make them seem cold.

Tough-hearted people do not necessarily have any intention of hurting others. They are simply emotionally detached and relatively unaware of how others are feeling. To get along with them, one has to start by accepting this reality, and then be willing to relate to them on their terms.

What are these terms that we need to understand in order to get along with the really tough-hearted? The most important thing to keep in mind is that they have very concrete ideas about which kinds of social behavior are okay and not okay. Rather than relying on empathy—on how something they do might affect your life, or how it might make you feel—in order to decide whether it is okay to do something, or to treat you in a certain way, they rely on set rules to guide them. These rules very much reflect the way they've been treated by others for most of their lives. If they've been treated with respect, and loved, that's one thing; but if they've been abused and neglected, that's quite another. In the former case you can expect even a fairly tough-hearted person to possess a sense of fairness and decency. They can be kind and considerate, because they learned that such behavior constitutes the social rules of the road. You may not be able to feel close to a person like this; on the other hand, you need not fear them.

Tough-hearted people who learned that abuse and intimidation are the appropriate rules of the road in dealing with people are an entirely different matter. No matter what they were *told* growing up, it is how they were treated that counts. You can expect them to treat you in this same way, and you are wise to be wary of them. In a relationship with such a person it will be up to you to establish new rules.

6

Insecurity: Inside and Out

Man's sphere is out of doors and among men—woman's is in the house—Man seeks for power and influence—woman for order and beauty—Man is just—woman is kind.

—RALPH WALDO EMERSON

To be sure, we no longer live in a world where women stay at home and men go to work, or where men compete for power while women seek order and beauty. The *jock* and the *entrepreneur* are our contemporary cultural heroes and role models—increasingly, for men and women alike. Even when they were written, though, it's for sure that these nineteenth-century notions of masculinity and femininity failed to account for individual differences in temperament and experience. Not all men—then or now—are as tough-hearted as these words imply; nor are all women as tenderhearted. Beyond that, simplistic sex-role expectations like these fail to take into account the impact of experience and temperament on the unique personality that each of us develops. For example, they do not take into account insecurity, or how it affects the way a person sees the world and reacts to it. Insecure men and women do not see the world, or relate to others, the same way that secure men and women do. Similarly, insensitive people see and react to the world in different ways than sensitive people do. That's the limitation of stereotypes: they fail to allow for the richness of differences in temperament and experience that ultimately form our personalities and make us unique. Instead of accepting their individuality, many people try to live up to the expectations that they think society has set for them, only to feel like failures when they can't.

Unfortunately, many contemporary books about men and women still seem to overlook the fact that real people aren't stereotypes. Instead, they continue to present us with broad generalizations about how men and women are, with little or no regard for how temperament and experience shape us as individuals. Today's stereotypes may be different from what people thought a century ago, but they are still stereotypes.

This book, and the theory of interpersonal sensitivity, is an attempt to move beyond the level of simple stereotypes in understanding men, women, and relationships. Of course, men and women *are* different. We know they are different anatomically and hormonally, for example; and it only makes sense that these kinds of differences will be reflected in some differences in behavior and temperament. It may also be true that we as a society continue to raise boys and girls in different ways, and hold different expectations for them. However, in many sectors of society, these differences are rapidly disappearing. In more and more communities, girls and boys are being raised to fulfill very similar expectations. Foremost among these expectations is to be a competitive person. We promote competitive team sports, as well as individual competition, for boys *and* girls, more than we ever have in the past. In doing so we are preparing them for survival in the global marketplace, with all that implies, including the ability to be mobile, to work long hours in a competitive atmosphere, and to share the economic load of contemporary family life.

Although insecurity often shows up somewhat differently in men and women, there are no simple stereotypes that we can use to describe insecure men versus insecure women. That is because factors like individual experience and differences in interpersonal sensitivity are so powerful, and must be taken into consideration.

In this chapter we examine insecurity "inside and out." We'll take a closer look at what goes on *inside* the insecure person. The *dynamics* of insecurity—what goes on on the inside—are very similar for men and women. In contrast, the ways in which that insecurity appears from the *outside*—in attitudes and behaviors—can be different for the two sexes.

INSIDE THE INSECURE PERSON

What is it like, on the inside, to be an insecure person? For one thing, the inner life of an insecure man or woman can be very different from what you see on the outside. What you may experience could very well be an attractive, competent individual; how they experience themselves, however, could be just the opposite. It's not unlike watching a river run: the turmoil beneath the surface may be nothing like the smooth waves you see rolling by on the surface.

Of course, some people reveal their insecurity for all to see, but more typically insecure people go to great lengths to conceal it. That's because they realize how different their private lives are from their public selves. Though they may be satisfied with, and even proud of, their public selves, it is their private selves that they want to conceal. Usually it is only those who are closest to insecure people who know how they really are.

First, insecure people are *self-conscious*. They are forever watching themselves with a critical eye. They are forever judging themselves, usually harshly, and worrying about how they will be judged by others. The self-doubt of insecure people runs so deep that they can rarely walk into a public place, attend a meeting, or strike up a conversation without being aware of how they might be perceived, and worried that they might do or say something wrong. The worse the insecurity, the worse the self-consciousness and the more self-critical the person is apt to be. Some might think this means that insecure people are selfish or self-centered, but this is not the case. They may in fact be self-absorbed, but that does not make them egotistical or vain. On the contrary, their self-consciousness causes them nothing but discomfort. Whereas the egotist watches himself and loves what he sees, the insecure person watches himself and worries.

As the word implies, inwardly insecure people are not confident. Even in the best of times their sense of confidence is easily shaken. They may be able to look at themselves and their lives objectively and find good reason to feel proud of their accomplishments. On this objective level, you could even say that their self-esteem may be good. The insecure man or woman may know very well what they've achieved, their talents and abilities. But they are always watching themselves; meanwhile, all it takes is the slightest criticism, disapproval, or perceived failure to set off intense feelings of anxiety. On the deepest level they aren't sure of their place in the world: their purpose in being here, their intrinsic worth as members of a community.

Insecure people are easily wounded, and once wounded they have a hard time healing. They mull over whatever it is that hurt or disappointed them. Those who are closest to them—their partners, to be sure, but sometimes also their colleagues and friends—may be aware of this. They experience the insecure person not only as thin-skinned but also as someone who doesn't let go easily of a hurt. Whether or not they want to admit it, the insecure person ends up harboring resentments toward those who've hurt them. They also experience the natural human urge to strike back. The ways in which they do this, however, may be obvious or subtle, direct or indirect. It can also be different for men and women.

Insecure people also have a hard time accepting normal human flaws and faults. Since none of us is perfect, all of us are bound to act in ways at times that can hurt or disappoint even someone we love. As anyone who's been in a relationship or had to work closely on a team with an insecure person can tell you, their sensitivity in this area can be very stressful. "I have to be extremely careful about how I approach Brett," one supervisor told me. "He's a very talented guy, but the work we're doing here is cutting-edge, and it's really impossible to get everything right the first time around. That's why we rely on a team approach, one hundred percent. Most people accept this. I have to take great pains, though, whenever I have to redirect Brett or accept another team member's recommendation instead of his. He never says anything, but you can see it in his eyes—the hurt and resentment. You can actually *feel* it!"

The problem, this manager explained, was that Brett's performance, and as a result the performance of the whole team, would usually suffer whenever Brett went into one of his moods. He'd noticed that others tended to be cautious around Brett as well, with the result that the team's productivity as a whole was being stifled.

This supervisor, knowing Brett to be a talented engineer, had no idea that his employee was also a very insecure man. What he did know was that it took extra time and care to handle Brett, that Brett was not what he considered a team player, and that his team's productiveness was suffering because of it. "Brett has this need to shine as an individual," he said. "He needs constant recognition. Sometimes I feel that he requires that even at the expense of the team. As talented as he is, there are definitely times when I feel that he's a liability. The problem is, I don't know how to bring this up without hurting his feelings again!"

I would predict that Brett's career will suffer sooner or later as a result of his insecurity. Many insecure people are like him: talented but thin-skinned and needing continual reassurance. Teams don't function well with one or more members like this among them. Often, insecure people find their careers being sidetracked without any clear understanding why. The most common reason is that their superiors find it easier to do that than to confront their insecurity.

***

Why do insecure people feel hurt so easily? Why would they have difficulty accepting the fact that even the best-intentioned people are bound to disappoint them, act thoughtlessly, or say something critical every now and then? To understand this we need first of all to appreciate just how much the expectations we hold influence the way we act. We develop our expectations from experience—the way we are treated growing up—and from modeling those whom we select as our everyday heroes. Most often these heroes are our parents, but they can also be someone else—a relative, a coach, a teacher. Finally, some of our expectations come from our unconscious. They represent wishful thinking of a kind.

Like everyone else, insecure people have expectations about the way they want to be treated and for how relationships should work. These expectations are usually so unrealistic that few if any people can live up to them. As a frustrated partner once said to me, "You'd have to be a saint to avoid hurting Jane's feelings or doing something to let her down. And I'm no saint!"

The unrealistic expectations of insecure people are usually the unconscious kind. Interestingly enough, *others* are usually more aware of them—and of how unrealistic they are—than the insecure person is. This was very true, for example, for Brett's supervisor, who was more aware of Brett's sensitivity to criticism and his need for approval than Brett was. Unfortunately, confronting insecure people about their unrealistic expectations usually only sets off their insecurity! It has to be done in a certain way, and not everyone wants to do that. I can't count the number of times that an insecure man or woman has reacted with absolute shock when I've suggested to them that they expect too much from other people or that they can be intolerant and unforgiving of normal human faults and flaws, including their own.

By unconsciously setting their expectations for themselves and others so unrealistically high, insecure people set themselves up for constant disappointment (from others) and a sense of failure (in themselves). They turn their relationships into self-fulfilling prophecies of disappointment and hurt. To make matters worse, for the most part they aren't the least bit aware that this is what they are doing. Beneath their insecurity lies the sensitivity they were born with. They may accept the idea that they are sensitive; but many insecure people have a hard time accepting the idea that they set their standards so high that others can't help but be wary, can't help but walk on eggshells around them, can't help but disappoint them. They also don't see their expectations for themselves as so unreasonable that they are bound to feel like failures.

So where do these unrealistic expectations come from? The unconscious expectations of insecure people have deep roots. They represent their way of compensating for whatever experiences they had in relationships that led to their being insecure in the first place. In other words, insecure people unconsciously seek to make up for whatever losses, abuses, or rejections they endured in the first place. Their hearts crave whatever love they lost or never had. Their wish—again, almost always an unconscious one—is to create an ideal relationship in which they are constantly loved and never subjected to abandonment, rejection, or abuse. This is what leads others to feel that they can never measure up to the expectations of an insecure person. Whenever I hear someone make this complaint—of feeling that no matter what they do, they can't measure up—I always suspect insecurity as an issue in the relationship. On occasion it happens that the person doing the complaining actually isn't trying very hard in the relationship; but it's just as likely to be the insecure person's expectations that are the problem.

OUTSIDE THE INSECURE PERSON

The ways in which inward insecurity appears in outward behavior can vary, depending on how severe the insecurity is and also on whether the insecure individual is a man or a woman. To illustrate these differences let's look at four different people: two men (one extremely insecure, the other not so) and two women, one of whom is also much more insecure than the other. Regardless of sex, however, one thing that insecure people have in common is that, despite how much they may want to be loved, it is not easy for them to open themselves to that love. The more wounded they are, the more distrustful they are, and the harder it is for them to let themselves be vulnerable enough to be loved. Their partners often report feeling shut out or pushed away by insecure people. As one woman put it, "There's a part of Ronnie that I can't get to. I don't think anyone can get to it. Sometimes I think it's his heart. It's just so guarded, so protected, that you can't really get to it, no matter how much you love him." Does this describe someone you love? Does it describe you?

* * *

Steve, the less insecure of our two insecure men, is twenty-nine and single. An attorney who graduated near the top of his class from a prestigious law school, for the past few years he's been doing what all aspiring young attorneys do: working sixty hours or more a week for a large law firm, hoping to be one of the few to be elected to partnership several years from now. He lives in a comfortable but tiny one-bedroom apartment on the East Side of Manhattan, overlooking the river. As he likes to joke about it, "The rent pays for the view, not the space."

Steve has been dating Joan steadily for two years. Because of his heavy work schedule, they get to see each other mostly on the weekends. And because Joan has a position as an account manager for an advertising firm, out-of-town travel usually eliminates one of those weekends each month. On account of this, their relationship has had to grow slowly. Joan has the feeling this is more okay with Steve than it is with her. She'd like to see the relationship move ahead, and ideally would like to be married in the next couple of years. She's twenty-eight, and her goal—which she has not yet shared with Steve—has always been to have a child at least by the time she's thirty-five.

Joan's attraction to Steve is based on her perception of him as a responsible, attractive man with a quick wit and a good heart. From the first time she met him she was impressed not only with his intelligence but with his consideration, his sense of humor, and his capacity to feel for his clients. Being a junior member of the firm, he gets many routine and low-fee cases, as well as some pro bono assignments. Rather than resent these as either small change or boring nuisances as many of his colleagues do, Steve always does his best with them, just as if they were high-paying corporate clients or complex, high-profile cases. Joan also appreciates Steve's capacity to have fun when he can. They both know how to let their hair down and how to leave work behind on a vacation. This has meant that they can play well together, and these times together are among Joan's most cherished memories. She can picture them being a happy family.

As much as she likes Steve and has positive feelings about their relationship, Joan also knows that beneath his success Steve is a troubled individual. She doesn't know much about insecurity or its causes, but she does know that Steve is very thin-skinned. He worries an awful lot, in her opinion, about what others think of him, and seems awfully hard on himself. In their relationship she's noticed that he avoids conflict at almost any cost. Joan finds this surprising, given Steve's profession. "Steve argues for a living," she told me. "In court he has to have skin as thick as an elephant's. But in our relationship he can't stand conflict. Even minor disagreements upset him. He avoids them like the plague."

More than once Joan has realized too late that some little comment she's made has affected Steve deeply. He's had similar reactions on several occasions when she forgot to do some little thing she'd promised to do, or said something that hurt him. In each of these instances Joan had no intention whatsoever of being thoughtless, much less cruel or hurtful. She either just got caught up in the business of her daily life and forgot to do something, or had simply spoken frankly without thinking too much about how Steve might react. Once, for example, she expressed frustration at the fact that Steve hadn't asked her to spend a weekday night together at his place in over a month, even though they lived only blocks apart in lower Manhattan. It was not until the next day that she realized, from the way he was acting, that something was bothering Steve. It took her a while to figure it out, because despite how he was acting, Steve denied that anything was bothering him.

Joan can tell when something is bothering Steve, she says, because he gets noticeably withdrawn and moody. He "forgets" to call and begs off quickly if she calls him. At these times it is clear to Joan that she is getting the cold shoulder treatment, though, again, Steve will deny this if she brings it up. Still, Joan is certain at those times that Steve is mad or upset with her. "It isn't what he *does*," she says, "but what he *doesn't do*. When he's hurt and angry he doesn't talk to me, doesn't seem interested in me, avoids me." In contrast, Joan is much more of an assertive person, expressing good and bad feelings alike fairly directly.

The most troubling aspect of Joan's relationship with Steve, though, is his attitude about commitment. Whenever she tries to bring up the issue, no matter how tactfully or gently, he clams up. The few times she's been able to get him to express some thoughts or feelings about their relationship and where it is going, his attitude has been pessimistic. "What if we lived together and after two years you decided you didn't love me anymore?" he once asked. And another time he asked: "What if we got married and ended up fighting all the time?"

Of course, it's normal to have concerns when we contemplate commitment. But the intensity of Steve's reactions, and the fact that the problems he imagined were so inconsistent with their experiences together, points to something deeper. Joan correctly suspects that these kinds of comments come from some deep wound in Steve's heart. But he never talks much about his growing-up years. She knows that his parents divorced when he was young and that he hadn't had much contact with his father after that on account of his mother having to move several times for better jobs. She also knows that Steve's first passion had been literature and writing, not law, but that he couldn't see his way clear to pursuing writing as a living. Beyond that he is pretty much of a closed book when it comes to talking about his past.

Steve is a good example of a man who suffers from what we could call moderate insecurity. He is self-conscious—worried about how others see him. His feelings can be easily hurt. He is also self-critical, frequently feeling that he isn't doing as well as he could. These feelings reflect the fact that he holds some pretty unrealistic expectations for himself and for relationships—expectations, moreover, that he isn't even consciously aware of. He holds on to his hurt feelings and has a hard time letting go of them. In part he has a hard time letting go of them because he doesn't express his hurt feelings directly. Similarly, he does not express his anger directly but withdraws his affection instead. He builds up stores of resentment—which he also holds on to—but denies it when confronted. He avoids conflict, but to do so he must also avoid being direct. That way neither his hurt feelings nor his resentment ever see the light of day. Instead, they fester, where they can eventually poison his relationship with Joan. He lets her know he's upset or angry only by withdrawing from her. He then relies on her to perceive what he is feeling and draw him out; otherwise issues between them might never get resolved. In time this will become a strain on Joan, who will either confront Steve about his passive aggressiveness or else build up resentments of her own.

Steve's approach to relationships is defensive and self-protective. He has a steady girlfriend who is committed to their relationship and loving toward him, but he limits their time together so that the relationship cannot deepen. His attitude about commitment is also a defensive one: his thoughts run not to what he might gain but to the possible ways he could be hurt or let down. This goes well beyond what we might consider normal concerns about commitment.

To deal with Steve's insecurity, Joan must first of all recognize it for what it is. It can be tempting—but wrong—simply to write off his anxiety as either an inability to commit or, perhaps worse, a sign that he does not really love Joan. The first interpretation unnecessarily pathologizes Steve; the second would cause Joan to conclude that something in her or in their relationship was lacking, which might not be true at all.

Recognizing insecurity opens the door to communicating about it, which starts the healing process. Clearly, this relationship has a lot going for it. It would be a big mistake both for Joan and for Steve to walk away from a relationship this promising. By recognizing Steve's insecurity, Joan can reinterpret some of his worries, putting them in their proper context—as products of his past, representing mostly fears of abandonment. Seeing them as an inability to commit or as a sign that he didn't love her would make Joan want to run away. On the other hand, by exposing such fears to the light of day, they can be interpreted for what they really are and be dealt with. Through an open and honest dialogue the reality of Steve's relationship with Joan can be compared to his past, and his irrational fears can be placed in perspective. The alternative, of course, is for these irrational fears to continue to control his behavior and poison his relationships, with Joan or anyone else. Communication also allows Steve (and Joan) to examine their expectations for a relationship and to sort out what is realistic from what may represent wishful but unrealistic thinking. Identifying unconscious, unrealistic expectations—for example, that a couple should never fight—opens these expectations to change. In contrast, so long as they remain unconscious, these expectations will control our behavior and drive our fears.

***

Mark shares some of Steve's traits, but in him they are carried to more of an extreme. This is because he is a much more wounded, insecure man. As a child he was teased and ridiculed constantly by his father and two older brothers, all of whom accused him of being a sissy because, unlike them, he was sensitive: he did well in school, was liked by his teachers, enjoyed reading and drawing, and didn't like to fight.

Mark's father was also physically violent with all of his sons. He was proud of being tough, and praised rather than scolded his sons when they acted the same way. "You've got to be tough to survive," was one of his favorite expressions. His sons—all except for Mark, that is—modeled his attitudes and behavior in their own lives.

Not once but twice Mark had fingers broken in altercations with his father. Once he'd suffered a cracked rib, and one of his eyebrows was split by a thin scar—the result of a beating with a broom handle. And he'd had his share of bumps and bruises from his brothers as well. Though his father had managed to avoid any legal consequences for his violence, Mark's brothers weren't so lucky. By the time they were eighteen both of them had been arrested more than once, and at the time we met, one of them was serving two years for assault. Mark, meanwhile, had never been in trouble with the law, had put himself through college, and was now making a good start on a business career.

Mark came to see me after two incidents in which he lost his temper with his fiancée, Kate. The first incident occurred when they argued over whether she'd been flirting with one of Mark's friends at a party. She denied it, but he'd exploded. For a moment she'd thought that he was going to assault her. He didn't do that; but he did rant and rave, raising his voice to a fever pitch. After the yelling stopped and the dust had settled, the next day Kate told Mark how frightened she had been. She'd never seen that side of him, she said, and she hoped she never would again. Things were tense between them for several days afterward. Mark apologized sincerely, Kate gradually let go of her fear, and their relationship seemed to return to normal.

A few months later, the second episode happened. This time Kate was not showing signs of recovering from it. This fight was over her parents, but the theme was the same: Mark felt jealous and threatened when he perceived that Kate's commitment to her family took precedence over her commitment to him. As is true in most of these cases, the actual event that precipitated the blowup was relatively minor: Kate had ignored Mark (from his point of view) at a big family gathering. Now, as a result of this latest blowup, Kate was talking about breaking up.

As was true for the first explosion, Kate didn't have an inkling that Mark was as upset as he was—until they were alone in her apartment afterward. Then, once again, the accusations flew. Mark's anger escalated quickly. No matter what she said, Kate could not calm him down. He shouted. He called her names. His face flushed red with rage. And then, in the process of storming out, he picked up a chair and smashed it against a wall. Pieces of chair flew, one of them knocking over a lamp, another striking Kate a glancing blow.

Mark's rage evaporated the instant he saw the piece of chair leg hit Kate. In that moment he also felt his stomach sink, as he saw the expression on her face and realized the potential cost of his latest outburst. He tried to apologize, but Kate would have none of it. She told him to leave, firmly and flatly, and refused to talk with him about what happened. He heard her bolt the door as soon as he was on the other side of it. For the next two days he was unable to reach her by phone. He got only her answering machine; and she didn't return his messages. He thought of going over, but then thought better of it.

Three days later Mark got a letter from Kate. His stomach tightened into a painful knot as he opened it. It was short. She wrote that she loved him very much but also that she was having serious second thoughts about getting married. She was still waking up at night with anxiety, and the idea of seeing Mark unsettled her. She asked him not to contact her—she would call him in a week or so. In closing, she offered two pieces of advice. The first was to not minimize or ignore this part of his personality. She'd seen enough of it, she said, to know that it could destroy any relationship Mark might have. Second, she urged him to see someone about it. She also knew the loving side of him, she explained, and she knew there must be some explanation for this other, dark side. She expressed the hope that whatever was causing his pain and driving his anger could be identified and healed. That's where I came in.

The first thing I discovered from talking to Mark was that he was indeed by nature a sensitive person who had had the misfortune to be born into an insensitive and violent family. It was that violence, combined with the continual ridicule he'd had to endure, that had been largely responsible for his becoming as insecure as he was. His brothers had also been brutalized, but as Mark described them it appeared they had much less sensitive natures than he. Consequently their lives had followed a different path, and they became violent men like their father. But Mark had done his best to contain his anger, as well as his pain. I also learned that Kate knew none of this. Both of Mark's parents had died before they met. He hadn't seen either of his brothers in years and didn't care to. Kate had noticed that whenever she tried to talk to Mark about his family or about growing up, he seemed uncomfortable and eager to change the topic. Like Steve, Mark preferred to try to bury his past and all the feelings associated with it. I have found that insecure men try to do this even more than insecure women do. Maybe we still hold on to some expectations for men to be emotionally tough—to bury their pain rather than express it—and maybe men still try to live up to these expectations.

I also noticed that Mark was uncomfortable talking about his family. Beyond that, I noted that at times he would go so far as to try to minimize the emotional impact that his violent youth had had on him. At one point he almost seemed to be trying to excuse his father's violence, or at least to deny its effects. "I think he really tried his best," Mark said. "I just don't think he knew how to relate to the world, or to his sons, any other way. I think he was trying to toughen us up because he really believed that you have to be tough to survive in the world." And was beating up your sons the best way to accomplish that? I asked. Is that how Mark would approach it, if he had sons? He turned red when I asked those questions, and looked away.

As for the effects of the violence on him, Mark had this to say: "I'm not sure how much it really affected me, really. After all, it was a long time ago. I haven't even thought about it in years." Once more it seemed to me he was trying to avoid facing reality—trying to minimize the effects that his violent youth had on his personality development. So I asked him how else he could account for this potential for violence in himself. Did he really think he was just like his father and brothers? Did he believe he acted like someone who'd been loved and nurtured through his formative years? And would he expect his own children to bear no scars if he treated them the same way he'd been treated? Again, Mark avoided looking me in the eyes and shifted in his chair. That session, as uncomfortable as it was for him, was actually the starting point for Mark's recovery from insecurity.

On the outside Mark was a bright, considerate, and successful young man; on the inside he was tortured by severe insecurity. In men this often takes the form of *pathological jealousy:* jealousy that can get so intense that it not only becomes irrational but can lead to violence. They are prone to becoming severely depressed over perceived rejections. Their depressions often baffle those who are close to them, who fail to see the supposed rejection at all. Kate was well aware of this tendency in Mark. In fact, his two explosive episodes were preceded by his suddenly slipping into a funk, which was her word for Mark's capacity to sink abruptly into deep depression, a dark mood that was much like the gathering clouds that darken the skies just before lightning strikes.

Severely insecure men can become very possessive in relationships. At the same time, those who love them often say that it is hard to convince them of their love and that very insecure men hold back on some level when it comes to giving their love in return. Their possessiveness, which in truth only reflects their intense craving for love and attention, often gets to the point where their partners feel smothered. The intensely insecure man just cannot bear the idea that he might lose the object of his love and the source of the love he gets. Like Mark, these men often choose affectionate, loving mates, only to drive them away with their jealousy, their insatiable demands for attention, and their possessiveness. This was certainly happening for Mark.

Thanks to Kate's advice, plus Mark's courage in seeking help, his story eventually had a happy ending, even though Kate did break up with him. He committed himself to the difficult work of looking at, rather than avoiding, his painful past. He reluctantly came to see himself as someone who'd been born with a sensitive disposition and who had become severely insecure as a result of abuse. He also came to accept the unconscious expectations he'd had for himself and, especially, for any woman who was in a relationship with him, and how no woman could realistically live up to those expectations. Gradually he began to look beyond whatever relationship he was in to meet all his needs for support, and to learn to love himself. At the point where he moved to another part of the country and we stopped working together, he was in a relationship that seemed much more balanced than any he'd had, with him providing as much caring and support as he was getting, and without smothering the woman who loved him.

* * *

Jill is our example of a moderately insecure woman. Like our other examples her insecurity is not obvious from the outside. Her friends would describe her as outgoing and active, fun loving and bright. She has a definite flair for dressing in ways that make the most of her good looks. Thirty-two years old, she's an accountant and likes her work very much. She shares a rented condo with her best friend, and loves to travel. She's a committed jogger and also enjoys biking and tennis. She doesn't lack for dates but has no steady boyfriend. Over the past year this has become somewhat of a concern. She's noticed that after getting off to a good start, all her relationships quickly fizzle out. The reason she most often gets from men when they break off with her is that they're not ready yet for a commitment and just want to date around. She suspects that these are excuses, but that's all they have to say. And then they don't call back. Her friends have reassured her, yet Jill also knows that most of them have steady boyfriends, and several seem well on their way to marriage.

Jill's greatest fault, those closest to her would most likely say, is that she has a definite tendency to be *defensive*. Although she does like to laugh, the boundary separating Jill's sense of humor from her defensiveness can be very fine and delicate. It is difficult, for example, to tease her, even gently, without her taking offense. And it's virtually impossible to say anything the least bit critical without upsetting her. This is because, privately, Jill feels that people don't take her seriously enough or value her enough. She often feels that even her best friends don't really listen to her or take the time to really understand her. In a word, she feels *misunderstood*.

People who work with Jill, including her supervisors, have also noticed her defensiveness. At team meetings, for example, she will usually respond to any comment she perceives as critical by launching into a long defense of herself. At such times her coworkers find it difficult to get a word in edgewise because Jill's defensiveness dominates the conversation. They have little choice but to sit and listen until she's done. Much potentially productive time is wasted in this way. Almost always, Jill's defenses of herself are unnecessary in the first place, since her colleagues actually have a high regard for her work. They also think of themselves as offering constructive suggestions, not destructive criticism; but Jill never takes it that way.

In her most recent evaluation, Jill's supervisor commented, "As you know, Jill, we all have to work as a team here, but frankly you often act as if it's your personal effort, and yours alone, that's on the line. You spend a lot of time and effort defending yourself. And you find fault with others. Your coworkers sometimes act like they have to walk on eggshells around you. That doesn't help us to work as a team. And frankly I don't think it helps you, either, Jill. I think it alienates you from the very people you need to rely on."

Her supervisor's feedback understandably stung Jill. To his credit, though, he was also one of the few supervisors who had the courage to confront an insecure employee. As I've said, too often insecure people find their careers being sidelined, but without any understanding of why—or of what they can do to change things. Because she perceived it as hard criticism rather than the constructive suggestion it was intended to be, Jill's first urge was to defend herself. At the same time she knew that, according to her supervisor, her defensiveness was the problem. So she bit her tongue instead of arguing back. But the comments disturbed her deeply. She mulled them over again and again. She lost sleep over them. What was most disturbing was that these words echoed something she'd heard from a couple of the men she'd dated. Until recently she'd discounted their comments, thinking they were just more evidence that people—especially men—didn't take her seriously. But now she was beginning to wonder if there wasn't a kernel of truth in what they'd said. Maybe she was, as one ex-boyfriend had said, her own worst enemy. Maybe she *was* too sensitive for her own good.

There's no doubt that Jill's insecurity has been causing problems for her. For one thing, it represents a threat to her career. Unless she is willing to look at herself and do something about her insecurity and defensiveness, she probably will not advance as she hopes she will. In her private life, meanwhile, insecurity has no doubt played a role in her relationships with men, all of which seem to end too soon and without any clear explanation. Ironically, her defensiveness may be the very reason why men leave her, and why their leaving has remained a mystery to her—it's too difficult to please Jill, and just too difficult to be frank with her. In that sense her supervisor's feedback could be the best thing that's happened to her in a long time. It just might open the door to self-examination and change.

In order to change, so that insecurity is no longer undermining her personal and work life, Jill needs to begin by changing her expectations for herself and others. Like all insecure people, inwardly she is incredibly self-critical. She is self-conscious and intolerant of even the smallest fault or flaw, and she gets really mad at herself for the slightest mistake. For example, she once told me that she was upset and angry at herself for an entire day because she'd failed to detect a typo on a memo she sent to her boss.

Jill's attitude about herself spills over into the way she approaches others. She's forever seeing a glass as one quarter empty instead of three quarters full. She knows that she tends to offend others at times by seeming picky, yet she can't seem to stop herself from finding faults and pointing them out. Predictably, this puts people off and makes them want to distance themselves from her.

In order to advance, Jill needs to become a more effective leader. She needs to learn how to motivate people. Naturally you can't do this very well by finding fault and criticizing. Anyone who's ever worked for a boss like that knows that it isn't motivating; in fact, most people in that situation look for another job. Effective leaders motivate through recognition and praise, and use criticism sparingly.

The work of changing expectations may sound easy, but as any insecure man or woman will tell you, it's not. Jill set herself to work on this, however. She used me, her counselor, as a sounding board and outside observer. We would talk about her experiences and encounters, both at work and in her personal life, with an eye toward her emotional reactions, and how these might relate to insecurity. This was not as difficult for me to see as it was for Jill. I knew, for instance, that being angry was almost always a sign that Jill was beating up on herself for some perceived mistake, which probably would turn out to be nothing much. I was also able to identify Jill's tendency to defend herself—I could literally hear her defensiveness in the pitch of her voice. Her defensiveness, I observed, was always preceded by anxiety.

In time, Jill began to become aware of these patterns, too. She learned to catch herself and to think before she responded. She learned to reevaluate her perfectionistic expectations for herself and was able to learn to be kinder to herself. This in turn led her to be less of a faultfinder with others. Last but not least, she worked on being able to listen to what others had to say without immediately interpreting it as criticism, feeling anxious, and responding defensively. This all took time, but from Jill's perspective the quality of her life was steadily improving, which made the effort more than worthwhile.

***

Jill's insecurity, as much of a problem as it is, is not nearly as severe as Claire's, whose life and relationships have been severely dysfunctional on account of it. Like Jill, Claire does not have a steady boyfriend; but unlike Jill's, the story of Claire's relationships is a story of continual conflict. Claire's boyfriends usually don't break off their relationship with her gracefully, as Jill's do; more typically they end in blowups.

Claire's insecurity is much more pervasive than Jill's. She is much more insecure, for example, about how she looks and what she does. She's forever watching herself, forever criticizing herself, almost mercilessly. At the same time she constantly seeks compliments from friends and boyfriends alike. She is so fretful about her looks and so obvious in the way she fishes for compliments that many people think she's vain and self-centered, when in fact she is self-conscious and insecure. While it is true that her insecurity causes Claire to be self-absorbed a lot of the time, her problem is actually that she thinks too *little* of herself, not too much.

Women rightly sense that Claire is competitive with them. She continually compares herself to them in looks, clothes, hair—in a word, everything. She's not above putting down other women when they are out of earshot—a habit that more than one friend has found irritating, thinking that Claire probably talks about them, too, behind their back. As a consequence of her competitiveness Claire has a hard time keeping close women friends. She's aware that many women don't like her, but she's blind to the role she plays in creating her own rejection. Like most very insecure people, her life is a self-fulfilling prophecy: she makes people uncomfortable and then feels rejected by them.

On the job Claire is inefficient. Though she is capable doing excellent work, her fear of doing something wrong causes her to procrastinate, missing deadlines. Her anxiety about how she looks causes her to be chronically late leaving the house, and therefore frequently late for work. Tardiness—often the kiss of death for anyone who aspires to advancement—has appeared as a problem area on more than one performance evaluation, and in more than one job. As with her relationships, Claire has left quite a few jobs on poor terms. This is truly unfortunate, because Claire is in fact a highly intelligent and talented woman; but as long as her coworkers and bosses see her as spacey and unreliable, her opportunities for advancement will be limited.

In her relationships Claire seems to be forever embroiled in conflict. In these situations she always sees herself as the victim. She contributes to their demise, however, by being extraordinarily defensive—much more so than Jill. Instead of merely feeling hurt easily and then defending herself, as Jill does, Claire takes on a more aggressive form of defensiveness. Whenever she feels hurt or offended by something that a current boyfriend says or does (which is often), she wants to talk to him about it incessantly. Invariably the man perceives this as hostile, for Claire is aggressive in her approach. It's obvious that she wants the man either to justify what he's said or done or to apologize. She presses for this very persistently. Of course, there is never a good enough justification, from Claire's point of view, for hurting her feelings. That leaves only one alternative: apology. Some men do this, at least for a while; but eventually every one of Claire's boyfriends has rebelled against having to apologize to her so often for offenses that they really felt were questionable. More than one has lost his temper. And though none of them, thankfully, has yet gone so far as to get physical, Claire experiences their anger as yet more abuse. She then tries to confront them about this, further fanning the flames. And so another vicious cycle gets started, and another self-fulfilling prophecy is the result. Claire's relationships end with the man in her life walking out embittered. She is not able to see this process from any perspective other than that of an innocent victim. Until she can, there's little hope for things to get better in her work life or in her relationships.

Claire's outward tendency to question others about perceived slights and injuries is mirrored by an inner tendency to find fault with almost everything about her and everything she does. Only those who are closest to her are aware of this. She perceives herself, for example, as fat and ungainly, socially awkward and boring. There is absolutely no balance in her self-perception, either: it is uniformly negative. She is self-conscious to an extreme, always monitoring herself for screwups. Naturally, she's always finding them.

Claire is a stranger to serenity—that sense of self-acceptance. Her approach to everything in life is colored by anxiety and doubt. Consider such a simple thing as exercise, for example. For Claire, exercise really has nothing to do with health, much less enjoyment; and it never leads to a feeling of satisfaction. She drives herself relentlessly, until her stomach is flat enough, her arms firm enough; yet she's never pleased.

This kind of chronic self-dissatisfaction in severely insecure women has a way of leaking out. Often it turns into chronic criticism of others. At the same time, severely insecure women like Claire are always worried about the status of their relationships. The idea that something might be amiss in an important relationship sets off panic in them. They obsess about it, just as they are inclined to obsess over perceived criticisms and personal faults. They are driven to make things right, even if that means driving others crazy by pursuing issues to death.

Not surprisingly, both Jill and Claire had experienced trauma in their early lives. This is true for all insecure people. All insecure people are born with basically sensitive temperaments. How secure or insecure they grow up to be depends on what kind of experiences they have. Sensitive people who are nurtured, loved, and respected grow up to be sensitive, caring adults. On the other hand, trauma can turn sensitivity into insecurity.

Between Jill and Claire, I felt that Claire was both the more interpersonally sensitive person and the more insecure one. It was no coincidence that she had also experienced the greatest amount of trauma. Both of her parents had been exceedingly critical, to say the least, singling her out from her siblings as the object of constant faultfinding. It didn't stop there, though. Both her father and her mother had been capable of sadistic meanness. Her father, for example, did not think twice about slapping one of his children for bad manners at the dinner table. He was unpredictable, and the children had to be careful what they said and did at meals. Claire's brother eventually became defiantly angry, and as a hulking teenager he'd finally put an end to this oppression by punching his father back, sending him staggering and drawing blood.

Claire's mother had been no better. No matter how brutal he was, she always sided with her husband. "You kids just have to learn manners," she'd say after he'd just finished slapping one of them around. And whenever Claire did something to displease her mother, she'd find herself locked in the basement for several hours. Claire, who'd been afraid of the basement for as long as she could remember—and who as an adult would do anything to avoid being in a basement—would huddle at the top of the stairs until the door was unlocked.

In comparison to Claire's experiences, Jill's upbringing was mild. She was the daughter of a minister who was somewhat vulnerable to fits of moodiness and whose work kept him out late four to six evenings a week. As a result he'd developed a lifelong penchant for afternoon naps. Jill described her mother as the "enforcer of silence." For years and years, Jill and her sister had to be absolutely silent when they came home from school, so as to not awaken their father from his nap. If that happened, the culprit would be scolded and sent to her room.

Worse than having to walk on eggshells around her father, though, was the fact that he had always seemed much more interested in his parishioners and in their children than he was in his own family. She described him as an absentee Dad and, in her more angry moments, as a hypocrite: "He was always there for the parishioners, twenty-four hours a day, seven days a week. He'd kiss their butts. If one of them called, he'd drop whatever he was doing. But he couldn't spare a minute for us. With us he was big on criticism but short on compliments." Beneath her anger I sensed a deep sadness in Jill: the legacy of never having been close with her father, at never feeling good enough to earn his attention or praise.

* * *

Perhaps you know a man like Steve or Mark, or a woman like Jill or Claire. Maybe you've been in a relationship with someone like this. Or maybe you even recognize some of these traits in yourself. These are insecure people who at heart are sensitive people and have a great capacity to feel and to give. That capacity lies buried, however, beneath their insecurity. But this does not mean that their situations are hopeless. On the contrary, it is possible to shed the burden of insecurity and to rediscover the sensitivity that lies beneath it. However, that journey needs to begin with insight. So long as insecure people persist in seeing themselves only as the victims of other people's meanness or thoughtlessness, indulge themselves in self-pity, and remain blind to the role they play in turning their lives into self-fulfilling prophecies, there is no opportunity for healing or renewal.

Growth requires that we find the courage to step back and see our situations in some perspective. Insecure people are often too caught up in their own anxiety to do this. In that sense a counselor can help. But insight does not *require* a counselor. All it really takes is an open mind. In my experience secure people can recognize not only their own basic sensitivity but also how it has evolved into insecurity.

OVERCOMING INSECURITY: FIRST STEPS

So, you've decided that you *are* a little insecure. Now what? you ask. What do I do about it? We'll be looking more closely at the issue of healing insecurity. As a preview, though, you can start thinking about three things.

Acknowledging Your Sensitivity

As obvious as this might sound, it's a step that some people have a difficult time taking. Men seem especially reluctant to admit that they are sensitive. Our culture still seems to promote the idea of men being strong and resilient, and somehow the idea of being *sensitive* is incompatible with that in many men's minds. Perhaps it's because they equate sensitivity with weakness. But sensitive men—Gandhi and Nelson Mandela are famous ones that come to mind—can also be morally strong.

I've encountered many women who do not like the idea of being sensitive, any more than many men do. They act as if it's offensive to them to be labeled that way. My impression is that they'd rather think of themselves as emotionally tough—sort of like the character Ripley, the heroine in the *Alien* movies. But in rejecting sex-role stereotypes, some women may be making the same mistake that men do in refusing to acknowledge the temperament they were born with. They, too, may be confusing sensitivity with weakness.

Identifying the Causes of Your Insecurity

Coming to terms with your own basic sensitivity can be a challenge in and of itself. The next step is to work through the pain associated with whatever trauma caused you to become insecure. Too often this pain is masked by anger, as was the case for Jill, who was angry at her father for taking an interest in everyone but her, but not very much in touch with the pain that was caused by their lack of a relationship. In other cases the pain is even more suppressed. Mark is an example of this. He actually tried to excuse his father's violence by writing it off as "just trying his best." That little mental trick kept him from feeling anything at all, either anger or pain; but it didn't really make the feelings go away, for they festered inside him. For him as for every insecure person, recovery starts with getting in touch with these feelings and then sharing them with someone you trust.

Seeing How Insecurity Is Poisoning Your Life

A third challenge for insecure men and women is finding the courage to look at how they may be contributing to their own misery. The truth is that insecurity causes people to hold many unrealistic expectations for relationships. Usually they are not even aware of these expectations or the fact that probably no one can live up to them. Mark, for instance, unconsciously wanted a partner who would make him the center of her universe. The minute he perceived Kate paying any attention at all to someone else—even her own family—he became pathologically jealous. Of course, there was no way that Kate (or any other woman) could satisfy his unconscious expectations. The only realistic choice was for him to become aware of them and change them. Only then would he be able to stop creating his own self-fulfilling prophecies in relationships, as all insecure people are inclined to do. The good news is that it is possible to reverse this cycle. It is possible for an insecure man or woman to replace the vicious cycle of unrealistic expectations, and the inevitable letdown they create, with a benign, or healing, cycle in which relationships begin to nourish them.

This is the way back from insecurity.

7

Emotional Predators

Jason sat across from me, slumped into the couch. His body language spoke louder than any words could. He'd been talking to me about his breakup with Leslie, a woman he'd dated for only a few months. They'd met on an airplane, both returning home from business trips. It would be fair to say that Jason had been smitten from the start.

"What do you think it was, about *you,* that attracted Leslie?" I asked.

"I know exactly what it was," he replied. "In fact, I asked her that very question."

"And what did she say?"

"She said she liked me because I was nice to her. She told me that she was struck by my kindness and good nature from the minute we first said hello. Also, she said she liked the fact that I *listened* to her."

The relationship had been short and intense. Jason emphasized that word—*intense.* "It was the most intense relationship I've ever had," he said. I was, of course, curious about what he meant, and I intended to find out.

"And what was it about Leslie that attracted you to her?" I asked.

"She's an incredibly intense, incredible powerful woman," Jason replied. "She's a corporate attorney, a self-made millionaire, I think, or close to it. She works directly for the CEO. She says he never makes a major decision without talking to her first. And I believe her. I've no doubt that she can dominate a corporate boardroom and make short work of virtually any opponent. She's truly brilliant, easily the most intelligent person I've ever known. Just incredibly sharp."

"Anything else?" I asked.

"Well, she's also very attractive. And sexual. Very sexual."

"So sex was good, and that was part of your attraction?" I asked.

Jason nodded. "Yes. I'd have to say that sex with Leslie was the best I've ever had. In a way, that is. I mean, it wasn't especially intimate. But it was . . ." He paused.

"Intense?" I offered.

Jason laughed. "Yes. You could say that."

"So," I asked, "were there any negatives?"

Jason grimaced. "Yes. Definitely. There were plenty of negatives. But I didn't see them at first. It's funny, but as intelligent as Leslie is, intellectually speaking, on an *emotional* level she doesn't seem very smart at all. What I mean is, she doesn't seem to understand—I mean, *at all*—how someone else is feeling. She can come across as very emotionally intense herself, but I can't tell you how often she was just plain insensitive to how I was feeling or to how her words or actions made me feel. Another thing—she knows what she wants, and she goes after it with gusto. And if what you want doesn't match what she wants, watch out!"

"Sounds like she could be overwhelming," I said. "Can you give me an example of this insensitivity that you're describing?" I asked.

"Sure," Jason replied, "Leslie always seemed genuinely surprised when she did something that hurt my feelings. She just didn't seem to understand why my feelings could be hurt. I can't ever remember her asking, even once, how I was feeling. She had no qualms about talking to me about her other relationships, either, or how I might react to that. I mean her sexual relationships. And she's had plenty of them. She'd just chatter away about all the different places she'd had sex, or who her best lovers were, and what they'd done together. Even after we'd just had sex. I don't think of myself as a prude, but I thought that was kind of insensitive of her. I have a lot of men friends and I don't think any of them would find it fun to have their wife or girlfriend talk about other lovers right after they've had sex. But when I said something about it, she just laughed."

"I see what you mean," I said. "And what about your other comment—about Leslie being aggressive, and what could happen if you and she didn't want the same thing?"

Jason gave a little snort. "She has a temper. A bad one. She can fly into a rage at any little thing. This happened a few times, even in public. At first I was baffled, unsure of what I'd done to set her off. But after a while I came to realize it was when she was feeling frustrated."

"You mean, when she wasn't getting what she wanted?"

"Yes. And it could be any little thing. I'll tell you, that temper of hers got me in touch with how formidable she could be. I wouldn't want to be one of her enemies!"

"I see," I said. "So, why are you still attracted to her?"

"What makes you think I still am?"

"Looking at you," I replied. "You look like you just lost your job, or your house, or something else very dear to you."

"I suppose you're right. I guess I do miss her. It's that intensity, I guess. She really is a very attractive, engaging woman."

"And intensely sexual," I added.

He laughed, blushing. "Yeah, that too. You know, it's kind of like being attracted to a tiger at the zoo. You know that this is no house cat. But it's so very intriguing, so seductive. You sense its power to destroy, and part of you feels the anxiety of that awareness. Part of you wants to run the other way. At the same time, you're drawn in by that very dangerousness. I think that's the way I felt about Leslie from the start. You're right: I still feel broken up about being rejected by her, even though part of me knows that's the best thing that could have happened."

Jason's analogy succinctly described the very dynamic that draws many sensitive men and women into relationships with *emotional predators.*

"Her insensitivity began to bother me more as time went on, and also her aggressiveness, which got worse. I'd tell her when she did something that hurt me, and she'd always act surprised. She really didn't seem to understand. It was like she was constitutionally unable to put herself in my shoes and understand how I might feel. She'd dismiss me, like I wasn't making sense or like I was making it up. At first I thought she was just being defensive, not wanting to own up to hurting me. But after a while I began to wonder if she really couldn't relate to how I was feeling. That made me uneasy."

The relationship also became more strained as Leslie became more aggressive. Jason described how Leslie would use aggression—including verbal and physical violence—to exert her will and get her way. "She can't seem to tolerate anyone opposing her," he said. "I thought maybe that was because she's worked for so long in such an aggressive, high-level, competitive environment—that she'd learned to be that way in order to survive. But after a while I began to think it was deeper than that—that it was something to do with her. From what I could tell from what she said about herself, she'd always been that way. You could call it strong willed, I suppose, but it's more than that. There were occasions when she'd just impulsively punch me in the arm—and not softly!—when she wanted her way and I was hesitating."

"Would you say that Leslie is someone who uses aggression regularly to intimidate others and get her way with people?"

"Yes. Definitely."

"Did her anger scare you?"

"Yes. In fact, I remember thinking once that she actually got off on it—frightening me, I mean."

"So, why did you hang in there?" I asked. "Why didn't you leave? Why was it she who broke it off?"

Jason turned his gaze downward and sighed. "I guess it's like I said: I knew I was playing with fire, but I was drawn to it. I think that part of me didn't want to believe that Leslie really was that way. I think I kept on looking for her soft side, even after I got burned, emotionally and financially."

"Financially?" I asked, surprised. "I thought you said that Leslie is wealthy."

"She is."

"So how did she burn you financially?"

"In a couple of ways. First, even though she'd boast about how much money she had—and lived a lifestyle to back it up—she never offered to share expenses, much less to pay. She has expensive tastes, too. She likes the best restaurants, the best bed-and-breakfast inns, the best wine. But she had no qualms letting me pay the tab."

"Anything else?" I asked.

Jason shifted uncomfortably in his chair. "She borrowed money," he said. "She once told me that she was unable to cash in some stocks for thirty days because it would cause her some problem with capital gains. There was some complicated reason I couldn't understand. I mean, I do okay, incomewise, you know? But I don't speak to my broker three times a week like she does. Anyway, she asked me if she could borrow five thousand dollars for one month."

"And you gave it to her?"

"Yes," he replied somberly.

"But you didn't get it back."

Jason shook his head. "She was supposed to pay me back in 'exactly thirty-one days.' Those were her exact words. But she broke off with me less than two weeks later. After another one of her tirades. That time we were in the middle of an art museum. She'd taken the program I'd been reading, and when I asked for it back a little while later she refused to give it to me. I asked her again if I could see it. I said I'd let her have it again when I was done. So, she puts the program behind her back—like a kid playing keep-away, you know? Only there was nothing playful about it. It made me uncomfortable. I didn't feel like playing keep-away in the middle of an art museum. But I could sense that she was taking some kind of pleasure in what she was doing. There was this little smile on her face. But it wasn't a happy smile. There was no joy in it. There was something about that smile that made me nervous."

"Did it strike you as cruel?" I asked.

Jason nodded. "Yeah. Now that you mention it. In a way, it did seem intentionally cruel. Like she was getting off on making me upset—on my discomfort. Anyway, I was pretty upset. We drove off in silence. I didn't feel like talking, to say the least. Then she asked me were we still going out for dinner. That's what we originally were going to do. Given what had happened, I couldn't believe she would have the nerve to ask me that! But she didn't seem to think anything of it. I said I wasn't feeling well and dropped her off. I knew she didn't believe me, but at that point I didn't care. Anyway, since then she's refused to answer my calls. I haven't talked to her in over a month. Technically you could say she still owes me the money, though my gut tells me I'll never see a penny of it."

Jason had gotten himself burned, all right. Like many sensitive people, he'd found himself in a relationship with someone who was just the opposite of him, in large measure because it was incomprehensible to him that someone like Leslie could really exist. Sensitive people sometimes are drawn to the very kind of person who uses or abuses them, either because they mistakenly see these people as strong or because they naively believe that there is a sensitive core beneath their insensitivity. Then again, sometimes it's the other way around: emotional predators often seek out sensitive people as prey. Whatever the reason, it seemed clear to me that Jason had been blinded by a combination of his own naivete, sexual attraction, and Leslie's charisma. The end result was that he felt exploited and deeply hurt. The most comforting words I could offer him were that, as compared to some people I knew who'd been in his shoes, he'd actually gotten off lightly.

***

Mary also made the mistake of getting involved with an emotional predator. She met Tommy at work. "He seemed bright, and he was very good with words, if you know what I mean" she said, "And handsome, too—I have to admit that." Mary knew that Tommy had a reputation for being a ladies' man, but she believed him when he told her he wanted to settle down.

They dated for only a short while before moving in together. That was when the trouble started. Mary described Tommy as someone who could not hold on to a dollar. She always knew he liked to spend money, but she had no idea, until they lived together, just how financially irresponsible he was. More often than not he was not able to come up with his half of the rent on time, so that Mary ended up paying the whole thing and waiting to be paid back. Of course, she waited and waited. Within a few months Tommy was in debt to her for well over a thousand dollars. Similarly, Mary found herself paying the utilities bills most of the time. What really irked her, though, was the way Tommy would ask her if she had any money whenever she suggested they do something, like dinner or a movie. "I was already paying most of the living expenses," she complained, "and then I'd have to pay for him to take me out! I told him that didn't feel very flattering."

"What did he say?"

"Oh, he'd just accuse me of wanting a 'traditional' relationship. He said he wasn't into being traditional. Got all huffy about it."

Before they moved in together Tommy had told Mary that he liked spending time with several male friends. He asked her if she would have any problem with that. She said no; on the contrary, she thought it would be good for him to keep his friends.

What Mary didn't expect was that Tommy quickly developed a habit of coming home two or three nights a week at two or three in the morning. The next day he'd say he'd been out with his friends. If she questioned him about this he'd get very angry. "You told me you thought I should have friends," he'd say. "And that's what I'm doing. What are you trying to do, make me into *your* idea of a boyfriend?"

The thing that Mary eventually came to like best about her relationship with Tommy, she told me, turned out to have nothing to do with him; rather, it was his family. In particular she liked his mother, and also his older sister and maternal aunt, who all lived together in a house not far away. Tommy's father had died when he was sixteen, and in the ensuing years the women had built a history together and developed close bonds. Mary found herself gravitating there, especially since there were so many nights when Tommy was out with his friends. She came to look forward in particular to Wednesday night dinners. They'd linger together, the four of them, over pasta and dark red wine, sharing the week's exploits, talking about topics ranging from the weather to raising children—something Mary had been thinking about.

In time Mary became quite attached to these women, and eventually she began to open up to them about Tommy. She was circumspect about this at first, not wanting to cause them any discomfort, but they were not tentative at all; instead, they spoke freely and uninhibitedly about the men in their lives, past and present. Tommy, she discovered, had always behaved in the family pretty much the way he behaved with her. "He's always been good at putting Tommy first," his sister said, and no one at the table argued.

Tommy's capacity for anger made Mary increasingly uneasy. It didn't take much to set him off. He could be vicious with his words, threatening in his demeanor. Any little complaint she'd try to express would be immediately turned into a complaint about her. He'd raise his voice, clench his fists, shoot a snarling look her way. It was a daunting prospect to bring up an issue with him.

Tommy, Mary discovered, was also a big tease, and there was an element of hostility in his teasing that disturbed her. For example, sometimes after getting home well after midnight (and when she was fast asleep) he would wake her up and want to make love. If she groggily said no, he'd rouse her by tickling her feet. He might do this three or four times. He seemed to find this very funny, she said, though it didn't amuse her in the least. The more upset she got, she said, the more pleasure Tommy seemed to get from doing it.

Mary was also a cat lover, and when she and Tommy moved in together she'd naturally brought her two cats. To her chagrin she soon discovered that he hated them. They'd been raised as house cats, and though curious about the outdoors, they were used to being outside only when Mary could watch them. But she found that she could not count on Tommy to make sure that they wouldn't get out; in fact, he seemed to leave doors and windows open all the time. He'd tease her about their getting lost whenever she was away. And once, when she came home unexpectedly, she was certain she heard him chasing them around upstairs.

Mary mentioned this last incident the next time she was at Tommy's mother's for dinner. "I swear I heard running upstairs," she said. "It sounded like the cats, then Tommy right behind them."

The response she got shocked her. "I think Tommy once took my cat and got rid of it," his sister said.

"What do you mean?" asked Mary, her stomach tightening into a knot.

"I had a cat once," his sister said. "When we were young. Tommy seemed to hate it, too, just like you say he hates yours. He teased it all the time—throwing it up in the air, pulling its tail. Kind of mean, you know? I thought he was doing it just to get me upset. Then, one day, the cat just disappeared. Tommy denied having anything to do with it, but I've always wondered about it."

That night when Mary went home she felt sick and couldn't sleep.

Mary hung in there with Tommy, even going so far as to talk about marriage, for the same reason that Jason had hung in there with Leslie. Looking back on it, she said, it was partly her sense of commitment that was responsible and partly her attachment to his family. "But it was also partly being naive," she said. "Part of me just couldn't accept that what I was seeing was real. Part of me kept thinking that there was a different Tommy—a 'real' Tommy, who was sensitive and caring—that would emerge one day." She gave up on that, though, when she happened to pick up the phone in their bedroom one Sunday afternoon at the same time that Tommy was answering it downstairs. He had no idea she was on the line, and she was about to hang up when she heard one of Tommy's friends say, "Are you coming tonight? Debbie and Carol will be there. Carol told Debbie she can't wait to see you again. She's really hot for you, man!"

That night Tommy went out. Mary kissed him good-bye. When he got home he found her and her cats gone, along with all the suitcases and most of her belongings. She left the furniture. She left no forwarding address or phone number. He never heard from her again.

THE PREDATORY PERSONALITY

As the above examples illustrate, two qualities that define emotional predators are their *lack of empathy* and their *capacity for aggression*. Emotional predators don't put themselves in another person's shoes— don't understand how the other person is feeling. Sensitive people who find themselves relationships with emotional predators often struggle to accept the fact that the other person doesn't understand how they feel. They either refuse to accept this reality or else cling to the idea that they will somehow be able to make the emotional predator into a sensitive, empathic individual. The truth is, though, that emotional predators are not in touch with how others are feeling.

Emotional predators also rely on aggressiveness a lot to get their way in relationships. This strategy is particularly effective with sensitive types, like Jason, who by their nature do not like aggression and who respond to it with a certain amount of discomfort and anxiety. But even less sensitive people respond to aggression with anxiety. The emotional predator senses the anxiety that aggression creates in others. However, since they don't empathize with that anxiety, there is nothing to inhibit them from using aggression to get their way. In time the emotional predator builds up a strong expectation that they can get what they want through intimidation. In many cases emotional predators will even find this process exciting. They take pleasure in inducing anxiety, which can lead some of them to become downright sadistic.

* * *

Sensitive people have a sense of right and wrong that is based not only on rules of behavior—on rights and wrongs—but also on empathy. Empathy—the ability to identify with another person's experience—is the basis for concepts like fairness and justice. Empathy allows the law to move beyond simple rules of right and wrong conduct to allow for extenuating circumstances. As everyone knows, juries decide guilt versus innocence, and also appropriate punishments, not only on the basis of objective rules but also on a subjective interpretation of those rules. The foundation for that subjective judgment is empathy.

For emotional predators, what is right or wrong behavior is based not so much on either rules of behavior or empathy; rather, it is based on *what you can get away with*. Simply put, if you can get something you want and avoid punishment, it's okay as far as emotional predators are concerned. Emotional predators are in touch with their own needs and desires. They are pretty much blind, however, to others' needs and desires. Their own needs always come first. If they do give, it is only in order to get something in return. If giving doesn't lead to getting something back, emotional predators get mad. For them, relationships are pretty much like refrigerators: something to go to in order to satisfy a need, and otherwise ignored.

Emotional predators are not unemotional. To a large extent they are in touch with their own feelings; and they definitely show emotions like excitement, pleasure, pain, and anxiety. It would be a mistake, however, to compare the emotional lives of emotional predators to those of sensitive people. The emotional life of the predator is limited and shallow compared to that of the interpersonally sensitive person. The emotional life of the sensitive person is rich and filled with complexity and subtlety. This is the result not only of their sensitivity to their own emotional states but of their sensitivity to the emotional states of others. As any sensitive person will tell you, how they are feeling at any given moment depends not only on themselves but on those around them. A happy moment that is shared, for example, is very different—for a sensitive person—from a happy moment that is experienced alone. Not so for the emotional predator, whose emotional life is defined solely by what happens to them and by whether their own needs are being satisfied.

Sensitive people are not angels. Sensitive people do wrong things just as anyone does. But sensitive people feel *guilt* when they do something wrong. Similarly, sensitive people can definitely do things that hurt another person's feelings. But when they do so, sensitive people feel some pain themselves. Emotional predators, however—because their morality is based exclusively on what they can get away with—do not experience guilt. Instead, they experience frustration when they can't get what they want. They can also experience anxiety when they are punished. When caught in the act of doing something wrong, the emotional predator may say they are sorry. This regret, however, is not based on empathy for someone they may have hurt, but on anxiety over being caught and potentially punished. If they aren't punished, they move on without giving a second thought to what they did.

***

One of the hardest things for interpersonally sensitive people to grasp is the idea that not everyone else is like them; and emotional predators are definitely not like them. In relationships with emotional predators, sensitive people almost always get exploited or abused. But sensitive types often wait and wait. For what? For the emotional predator to show some signs of sensitivity. Most often it takes some experiences of being burned, as happened to both Jason and Mary, before a sensitive person may conclude that the only sensible alternative is to terminate the relationship. Even then, sometimes it's the sensitive person—as in Jason's case—who actually gets dumped. Only later may they realize that this was the best thing that could have happened to them.

***

Much more common than emotional predators are people who are simply interpersonally insensitive, but without the added qualities that make emotional predators so dangerous to get involved with. Being in a relationship with someone who is different from you, in terms of interpersonal sensitivity, is an issue, but a manageable one. Being in a relationship with an emotional predator, however, is not really manageable.

COPING WITH AN EMOTIONAL PREDATOR

If you have ever been in a relationship with an emotional predator, or if you feel that you may be in one now, there are four things to keep in mind.

· **Look at this relationship** as it really is, instead of how you would like it to be. This is the first and foremost rule when dealing with this kind of person. Come to terms with the fact that people differ in interpersonal sensitivity. The range of interpersonal sensitivity is large. Some people are so sensitive that they seem to feel everything that others around them feel. At the other extreme, there are some people who *totally lack* the ability to empathize. Accepting this reality will make it easier for you to decide what to do. Although you may be able to put yourself in the predator's shoes and experience how you think they are feeling, don't assume that's really how they are feeling. And don't assume that they can relate to what you are feeling.

· **Set firm** *limits* for what is acceptable and unacceptable behavior, and make these limits clear to the predator. When your limits are violated, respond with some form of consequence, every time. For example, if you have a financial agreement, as Mary and Tommy did, but your partner has consistently broken that agreement, it's time to end it, or at least suspend it for a time, even if your partner protests. Lending more money today to a partner who just last week failed to meet a financial obligation will only perpetuate the problem.

· **Stand up to aggression.** Emotional predators learn that being aggressive often gets them their way. They rely on others' anxiety as the key to getting their way. Naturally, physical abuse should not be tolerated at all. That should be grounds for any sensible person to leave. However, many emotional predators use verbal aggression as opposed to physical aggression to dominate a relationship. If you are sensitive and tend to respond to aggression with anxiety, you will need to learn to desensitize yourself to some degree in order to survive in a relationship with an emotional predator. If you do not, your self-esteem will surely erode and you will find yourself being a victim time and time again. Stand up to aggression. *Do not confirm a predator's expectations by giving him what he wants because he gets aggressive.* Standing up to aggression does not necessarily mean fighting back, but it does mean standing your ground. It means not giving in to an emotional predator just to avoid their anger, for that will only reinforce aggressiveness. Remember: you don't have to yell and scream—just don't give in. It's always wise, of course, to be prepared with an escape plan in the event that verbal aggression does ever lead to physical violence.

· **Look after your own interests.** You can count on the emotional predator to do just that, so do the same. You definitely cannot count on anything like altruism here. The predator gives only in order to get. That might not be a fun way to live, but if you adopt this same attitude you can help to keep yourself from getting exploited too often. Keep some sort of ongoing balance sheet, and make sure you ask for and get something in return before you keep on giving to a predator.

The above guidelines can help you to survive if you are in a relationship with an emotional predator and feel that you must endure it. Keep in mind, however, that these relationships are usually very damaging to your self-esteem. In time you may find yourself feeling worn down and depressed. You may come to believe that you have little to offer or are not worthy of being loved. If it comes to that, the only sane alternative is to consider leaving.

8

Tender Hearts Together

In this chapter we look at some of the potential pitfalls facing two sensitive people who form a relationship. Many people might be surprised that there should be any such pitfalls. They might expect that a match between two highly sensitive people would be ideal—a match made in heaven. But is this really true? The answer has to do with several factors, the most important of which are

just *how sensitive* each person is

just *how insecure* each person is

Interpersonal sensitivity is a trait that can certainly enhance an individual's life. The capacity to empathize enriches our experience. Sensitive people are open to a great range of emotions, and they live a rich and complex emotional life. You might think of someone who is interpersonally sensitive as possessing a fine musical instrument—a violin, for example. Such an instrument not only plays music, but in the right hands it is blessed with great range and depth. As far as interpersonal sensitivity goes, those right hands are someone who is sensitive and secure. Insecurity makes it more difficult for sensitive people to use their sensitivity to their full advantage; conversely, conquering insecurity helps people discover the richness that sensitivity can add to their lives.

The emotional life of sensitive people is very much influenced by those with whom they share experiences. A laugh, a moment of sadness, or feelings of joy that are shared with a sensitive friend or partner is a very different experience, for a sensitive person, from one that is either experienced alone or shared with someone who is insensitive. Shared sensitivity amplifies our emotional experiences, adding complexity and depth to them. In contrast, nothing can be as frustrating to a sensitive person as trying to relate an experience or share one with someone who is very insensitive. Still, depending on just how sensitive a person is and how insecure they might be, sensitivity can have its pitfalls.

HYPERSENSITIVITY: WHEN YOU'RE TOO SENSITIVE FOR YOUR OWN GOOD

Can there be a downside to interpersonal sensitivity? Is it possible to be *too* sensitive? Interpersonal sensitivity is a dimension, varying from one extreme to the other. At one extreme are people who seem unable to empathize with others at all. Some of these people become *emotional predators*. Then there are the opposite: those who are acutely sensitive and empathic. We can call these people *hypersensitive*. If you have ever known anyone whose sensitivity was at this extreme end, you will know that the answer to the question "Can you be too sensitive for your own good?" is yes.

Hypersensitive people can find themselves unable at times to separate their own emotional experience from the emotional experience of those around them. Their emotional lives, in other words, often *mirror* the emotional lives of others, especially those they are closest to. This may not be so much of a problem when it comes to emotions like happiness and joy; it can be a big problem, however, when the person they are mirroring is experiencing pain, anxiety, or grief. At these times the sensitive person also sinks into these emotional states. Worse, they can remain stuck there for as long as the other person remains stuck there. Faced with this situation, an acutely sensitive person will usually try to make things better—to relieve the other person's grief, distress, depression, or anxiety. If they are successful, fine; but what if the person they are trying to help *chooses* to remain unhappy (or anxious, or depressed), for example by doing nothing to improve their situation? In that case the sensitive person is pretty much helpless. Unless they recognize the causes of their predicament (their own acute sensitivity and their inability to separate their own emotional experience from that of others) and actively work to do something about them, hypersensitive people can become the prisoners of their own capacity for empathy. If anything qualifies as being *too* sensitive, surely that is it.

Hypersensitivity can also inhibit a person from asserting his or her own needs. How? Out of fear of hurting someone else. Hypersensitive people would rather go without having their needs met than risk asserting themselves in order to ask for something that might cause even the least bit of discomfort, or arouse even a little distress or anger, in someone else. Like it or not, life requires us at times to assert ourselves, and to risk making someone else uncomfortable or angry, in order to get our own needs met. Even the happiest couples can tell you this: the key to a successful relationship is not that you never disagree or never have competing needs or interests; rather, the key is that you approach these issues with mutual respect and a willingness to listen and to compromise. But the hypersensitive person is so hesitant to put anyone out, so reluctant to make anyone uncomfortable, much less angry or irritated, that they don't engage in this kind of process. As a result they don't get very many of their needs met. Their self-esteem erodes and feelings of worthlessness eventually settle over them. Deep down they can also feel sorry for themselves and resentful toward others. Their self-pity, of course, comes from the fact that they don't get what they want, while their resentment comes from the fact that many hypersensitive people indulge themselves in secret expectations that others should know what they want, and give it to them, without their having to ask. Naturally, neither of these attitudes makes for good relationships.

Probably the best thing that can happen to a hypersensitive person is to establish a close, loving relationship with someone who is fairly sensitive. A sensitive partner is likely to be at least somewhat aware of their partner's feelings, and they are likely to use that awareness to try to figure out and satisfy at least some of their partner's needs. Even so, relationships with hypersensitive people are not easy. Their partners often complain about the fact that hypersensitive people have such a hard time expressing their needs and asserting themselves. This can be extremely frustrating. "I never know what Jane wants," one husband complained. "There are times when I sense that she wants *something,* or even that she disagrees with me about *something*. But it's like pulling teeth to get her to open up. It's hard to figure out what she wants, what she's really thinking. If I happen to figure out her needs, great; I feel like I've won the jackpot. I love Jane, and I like to make her happy. But I'm not a mind reader."

You could say that Jane was fortunate to be married to a man who put effort into trying to discern what she needed, instead of her having to assert herself. Of course, it is equally likely that a hypersensitive person like Jane will get into a relationship with an insensitive partner. That can be a pretty disastrous situation for the hypersensitive person. Invariably the hypersensitive partner in these relationships ends up getting very few of their needs met. When it comes to asserting their needs, they hold back. And they can't rely on a sensitive partner to try to figure out their needs, because they don't have one. In time they come to feel invisible. And they feel the way you might expect an invisible person to feel: depressed, worthless, and hopeless.

It can be tempting to blame an insensitive partner for a hypersensitive person's unhappiness; but in reality the hypersensitive person is equally responsible. They create their own misery by being so reluctant to express their needs and pursue them through a process of assertiveness and compromise. In order to improve their situations, hypersensitive men and women can't afford to wait for others to change. If their partner, for example, is relatively insensitive, it will do them no good to wait for that person to become sensitive. And if they are fortunate enough to have a sensitive partner, they still need to face up to the reality that the relationship may fail if they expect their partners to be mind readers.

Two people cannot have a successful relationship unless they are willing at times to have their feelings hurt, to learn to accept and deal with conflicting needs and desires, and to be assertive and learn to compromise. Hypersensitive men and women need to accept this reality and work to change *themselves* if they hope to have successful relationships. They may not be able to change their basic nature, but they can take responsibility for it, and they can learn to manage the way they respond to others.

WHAT TO DO IF YOU'RE HYPERSENSITIVE

If you think this description of hypersensitivity may describe you, here is some advice about the first steps you need to take in order to prevent your acute sensitivity from undermining your relationships.

· **Take responsibility for your hypersensitivity.** Don't blame others for being insensitive if you are, and always have been, a hypersensitive person. Use the material in this book to assess your own sensitivity as well as the sensitivity of those you are close to. Where on the dimension of interpersonal sensitivity do you and they fall?

· **Remember the saying that goes, "You can't make an omelet without breaking some eggs."** Assert yourself. Asserting your own needs and feelings may not be easy for you. It might make you uncomfortable. The other choice, however, is for those who are closest to you to know what you want and feel without your having to say so. Can they become mind readers, or should you begin to express yourself? Asserting yourself and expressing your true feelings may also mean that you sometimes disagree with someone close to you, that you ask them to go out of their way for you at times, or even that you hurt their feelings. Take a good look at these people. Do any of them seem to be made of fine china? Are they likely to break under any of these circumstances? Your first steps toward coming out of your shell may not be easy, but you need to take them if you want to break free of hypersensitivity.

***

Hypersensitivity is just as much of a handicap in the workplace as it is in intimate relationships. In fact, it can be worse, because whereas a partner may feel obligated to put up with hypersensitivity—to try to figure out what their hypersensitive partner wants, for example, and give it to them—coworkers, colleagues, and supervisors usually feel no such obligation. In fact, they usually learn to avoid hypersensitive people, making them all the more isolated and unhappy.

At work the hypersensitive person's emotional life mirrors that of those who are around them, just as it does at home. In some workplaces the emotional atmosphere may be relatively calm and peaceful. In many contemporary workplaces and corporations, however, the prevailing emotional climate is anything but that. A very common corporate climate today is something that has been described as *hard core*. It's a term that speaks for itself. Most companies today see themselves as struggling to survive in a competitive global marketplace. Prosperity requires eternal vigilance and aggressiveness. Accordingly, the atmosphere in these corporations is anything but serene. They expect their employees to embrace this survival ethic and to become comfortable with the hard-core corporate climate. Under these circumstances hypersensitive people are apt to become paralyzed. They absorb the stress of the hard-core environment, often taking it home with them at the end of the workday. This makes them vulnerable to getting sick, emotionally and physically.

The advice given earlier for the first steps that a hypersensitive person needs to take in his or her relationships applies to the work environment as well. Aside from that, my best advice to hypersensitive people is to avoid work environments that are hard core. Again, complaining about that kind of environment or expecting it to change in order to accommodate the hypersensitive person is unrealistic. Moreover, in that situation a hypersensitive man or woman is pretty much doomed to failure. These are people who are not just empathic but who feel every little anxiety or pain in others as if it were their own. They simply cannot bring themselves to be sufficiently competitive to succeed in the hard-core world, because being competitive means that when someone wins, someone else loses. This is true even if you are part of a winning team, since somewhere out there is a losing team. Hypersensitive people do best if they can somehow find or create a work environment that maximizes collaboration and minimizes competition. Of course, this is pretty rare. I usually advise hypersensitive people to choose a career and to search out a workplace that will take advantage of their empathic qualities, or at least not harm them. Certain types of counseling professions, for example, or self-employment as a skilled service provider, or as an artisan, may represent occupational havens for hypersensitive people.

INSECURITY AND COMMUNICATION

Two sensitive people who form a relationship need to be aware of certain potential issues if their relationship is to succeed. In general, though, their situation is usually more workable than what faces the hypersensitive person. The main issue in a relationship between two tenderhearted people is *communication;* or to put it another way, the main problem that can creep into and potentially destroy such relationships is *lack of communication*. Sensitivity—being in tune with each other's feelings—can truly make such relationships a joy. On the other hand, becoming afraid to express feelings will eventually lead them to ruin.

The most common reason for a breakdown in communication in a relationship is insecurity in one or both partners. As the following example shows, insecurity is not something that rears its head all the time. Many people are not burdened by really intense insecurity; by the same token, many of us are insecure enough that something can set our insecurity off. If that happens, there is a risk that communication in our closest relationships may break down.

Max and Jessica had been married for twelve years and had two children. Theirs was one of those marriages that most people initially thought would never succeed. Max dropped out of high school and went to work when Jessica got pregnant. They were sixteen at the time. She stayed in school and finished her junior year less than a month before giving birth.

For the next six years they lived in two large, hastily finished rooms in Jessica's mother's basement. It wasn't luxurious, but it was cheap. Jessica was extremely energetic, a naturally upbeat kind of person. She quickly made their modest place as homey as one could expect, and then some. After giving birth she returned to school, finished her senior year, and graduated with good grades. Max, meanwhile, had never liked school much to begin with, and said he'd rather work. He only reluctantly went to night classes to get a GED after his boss pulled him aside and told him he'd never get ahead without at least that much education.

Despite the odds against them—youth, early pregnancy, lack of education, and relative poverty—Max and Jessica made a success of their marriage. Max was hardworking and reliable, naturally bright, and blessed with good people skills. Staying at the same manufacturing company that had first hired him, he gradually advanced, working his way up from general handyman and company gofer to a successful sales position. Jessica worked part-time, taking only a short break to have their second child. Over six years they were able to save enough for a down payment on a home. It was small, but relative to what they started out with, it was luxurious.

For the next four years or so Max and Jessica were happy. They enjoyed their home, adored their children, and loved each other. People who knew them well saw a contented couple and a happy family. Max and Jessica were affectionate with each other, had shared goals, and worked effectively together to achieve them.

Trouble began to creep into this happy scene when Jessica decided to start college part-time. Max, though he personally still did not even like to read very much, except perhaps for an occasional newspaper, was supportive of what Jessica wanted to do. So Jessica started off on her higher education with enthusiasm. Unknown to both her and Max, though, this decision would soon set off a deep insecurity in Max, with potentially disastrous consequences for their marriage.

Why should something positive, like a decision to further your education, threaten to disrupt a happy marriage? Some might wonder whether it was an issue of control. Did Max think that education would somehow make Jessica harder to control in some way? And was being in control in the marriage an issue for Max?

The tendency to see every marital conflict as an issue of control has become very popular. But it is often wrong. In this case, too, it was wrong. Max and Jessica had already established a good balance of power—if by power we mean decision making—before any problems surfaced in their relationship. Max truly respected his wife's academic interests, even if he didn't share them.

The root cause of the problem that troubled Max and Jessica's marriage was not control but Max's insecurity. The symptoms of his insecurity included a definite tendency to withdraw, to become depressed and uncommunicative, and to be irritable with Jessica and the children. Also, although he'd always been a mild drinker, as was Jessica, as his insecurity made itself felt, Max started drinking more.

Like most insecure people, Max was unconscious of the fact that what set off his insecurity was a feeling of abandonment. Neither he nor Jessica made this connection, though, since in no objective way could you say that Max was being abandoned. After all, the only change in his life was that his wife was now at school two nights a week, in class, and in the local library most Saturdays, working on papers. But when it comes to insecurity, abandonment is in the eye of the beholder.

Why was Max insecure? And why did his insecurity come out only when Jessica decided to go to college? To understand that, we need to look only at the most practical impact of this decision. Again, that meant that Jessica and Max would be away from each other on a regular basis more than they'd ever been. She had her classes at night, because she still worked part-time during the day. This was a time when she and Max and the children would normally be home together. Also, because Jessica had to spend a lot of her weekend time at the local library (because being at home meant constant interruptions from the children), she was again away from Max more than he'd ever been used to. Back when she was completing high school, for example, he was at work while she was in school, and they spent all their evenings and weekends together.

I have seen it happen again and again: insecurity in a basically sensitive person can be masked by a caring relationship. In Max's case his insecurity had not become a problem for him or a threat to his marriage because he'd been fortunate enough to marry a caring, affectionate, and sensitive woman. Jessica knew from the time she first dated Max that he liked her attention, that he soaked up her affection. She also knew that he was not the most self-confident man in the world, although with her support he'd done all right for himself. Still, she knew that he liked it best when they were together and that he was always at least a little unhappy whenever they had to be apart.

Max's insecurity had its roots in a childhood that was marked by instability and separation. His own father had struggled with his career and as a consequence had moved his family more times than Max could remember, and even after the family would move, Max's father would spend three or four days a week away from home. So Max never established a strong connection to his father.

The two strong attachments Max had when he was growing up were to his mother and his older brother. His mother had told him more than once that he'd been a clingy child, who cried more than his siblings did when it came time for him to start kindergarten and who seemed to find more excuses than they ever did for staying home from school. Then, when he was barely seven, Max's older brother joined the military and left, pretty much for good. Up until then Max and his brother had been inseparable, and the loss was truly devastating for young Max. He developed acute anxiety, started wetting his bed, and sometimes refused to go to school.

A school psychologist diagnosed Max's problem as "school phobia." He advised Max's mother to accompany the boy to school and then leave him there, no matter how much he protested. Unfortunately, this psychologist had focused more on the symptom than the cause, and although Max eventually stopped protesting about having to go to school, his grief and anxiety, instead of being healed, merely went underground. He swallowed his sadness and expressed his pain and anger through problem behavior. He became somewhat rebellious, and he developed an antipathy for school that never left him.

INSECURITY AND THE WOUNDED HEART

Woundedness and anger lie at the heart of insecurity, and they reemerge whenever insecurity is set off. What you could call the *insecurity cycle* looks something like the diagram on the next page.

This cycle follows basically the same course in every insecure person. It begins with the *woundedness and anger* that created the insecurity in the first place. Later on we'll see that loss and separation do not necessarily have to lead to insecurity, if they are handled appropriately. Parents of sensitive children can minimize or even prevent their chil-

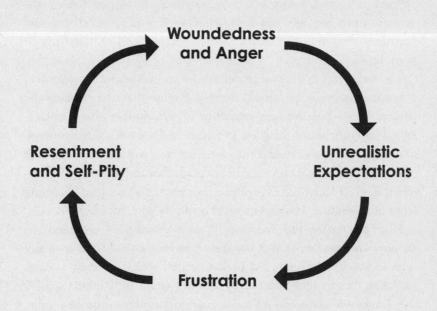

dren from becoming insecure. But in many cases, as in Max's, the effects of repeated losses and separations on children are underestimated. Because they learn to hide their pain and anger, it's often mistakenly assumed that these feelings go away. In fact, the emotions that lie at the root of insecurity merely go underground, where they sit, ready to reemerge at any time. All it takes is the right circumstances. When Jessica started college classes at night, spending evenings and Saturdays in class or the local library, instead of at home, Max's insecurity emerged.

The next step in the insecurity cycle happens when the insecure person comes to hold *unrealistic expectations* for others, especially for their closest relationships. In most cases these expectations are also unconscious. Max, for example, was not aware of how much he'd come to expect Jessica's constant company, support, and attention. These were things she'd given him, and gladly, from the beginning of their relationship, and that she felt she had gotten in return. Max had made no connection at all in his mind between his expectations for Jessica and the loss of her attention and the broken connections he'd suffered as a child. Jessica was puzzled when she sensed Max withdrawing from her. She was hurt when he began to be critical and impatient. And she was alarmed when she noticed him starting to drink more.

The next stage in the cycle is defined by *frustration*. The insecure man or woman harbors expectations for relationships that simply cannot be satisfied. This is because their unrealistic expectations represent *compensations*, unconsciously designed to make up for some earlier wound. Max expected Jessica to make up for what, as a child, he either hadn't had or else had lost. Again, he'd never made this connection on a conscious level. What he did experience, though, was a strong and growing sense of frustration. He knew he was unhappy with his life.

From frustration the insecurity cycle progresses to *resentment and self-pity*. This was what was beginning to happen to Max. In many ways it was like he regressed back to childhood, becoming anxious and clingy, and angry and full of self-pity when he couldn't get his way. Luckily for him and Jessica, though, the cycle was broken there, before he could sink too deeply into either self-pity or resentment and before the cycle could repeat itself and deepen. Not coincidentally, both of these emotional states are open invitations to substance abuse. This is in fact how many addicts begin their drinking or drug-using careers. Max could well have been another one of these, had the cycle not been broken.

The insecurity cycle does not truly end; instead, if unbroken it tends to repeat itself, only on ever deeper (and more dangerous) levels. The insecure person who falls into resentment and self-pity feels even *more* wounded than they did when the cycle began. From there, the cycle repeats itself. With each repetition of the cycle, insecurity worsens. Communication in relationships degenerates. The insecure person becomes more and more withdrawn. Irritability and unhappiness deepen, and substance abuse can increase, possibly advancing all the way to addiction.

To his credit, Max was open minded enough to give some serious consideration to how he'd gotten into this place where he was feeling deeply unhappy and frustrated, but unable to name the reason, and where self-pity and resentment were driving his desire to drink. Of equal concern to him was the deteriorating state of his marriage and his relationships with his children. He was fortunate, too, to have a loving partner who was willing to help him work through this crisis.

In the end, Jessica did pursue her education, and with the enthusiastic support of her husband. At the same time, she and Max made and kept a commitment not to allow their relationship to deteriorate as a result of the many other commitments that faced them, including work, children, and school. Jessica had no problem giving Max that extra attention he needed now and then. In turn, Max helped out more with the children, so that Jessica could study more efficiently at home, instead of always having to retreat to the local library. Last but not least, Max expressed his willingness to confront his own insecurity and to work through the grief, the woundedness, and the anger that he'd bottled up so many years before.

DANGER SIGNS

Couples who are aware of the dangers of insecurity and who work together to keep it in check will find that the channels of communication in their relationship remain open. Their shared sensitivity will bring all its blessings to them, enriching their lives both individually and together.

To make sure that communication remains open and that insecurity is not a threat to your relationship, here are some danger signs to watch out for:

✓ You feel that no matter what you do or how hard you try, you can't seem to satisfy your partner anymore.
✓ Your partner has become increasingly withdrawn.
✓ Your partner, who used to be very positive about you, has begun to be critical and irritable.
✓ Your partner seems to be feeling sorry for themselves, and resentful instead of supportive of you.

It's important to keep in mind that all of the above signs have meaning only in a certain context, which is that *things haven't always been that way*. In the case of Max and Jessica, for example, although Max showed all of the above signs, there was a period of many years in which he was not that way. This issue of context is important because it can help you to decide if something has happened that is bringing up some buried insecurity now. The alternative, of course, is that insecurity has been active since the beginning of a relationship. In that case your partner will have *always* been this way. That kind of insecurity is more difficult to deal with, because unlike Max and Jessica's relationship, in which they had good times to look back on, relationships that are burdened with insecurity from the start have no such context by which to gauge where they are now. They are faced with the daunting task of identifying and healing insecurity *before* they can begin to reap the benefits of a communicative, intimate, and mutually sensitive relationship.

* * *

All things considered, a relationship between two naturally sensitive people who both have an eye on their potential for insecurity and who share a willingness to work it through, if and when it does rear its ugly head, has the potential to be emotionally rich and fulfilling. It is a sad thing to see relationships with such potential fall victim to insecurity. Too often the causes for a breakdown in communication, which is one of the surest symptoms of insecurity at work, are misunderstood. That leaves a couple at sea when it comes to finding solutions that will help them either recover the intimacy they lost or else open the way to a new potential for intimacy. Very often it is insecurity—either ongoing insecurity or some dormant insecurity that has been aroused by a change in circumstances, as in the case of Max and Jessica—that is the culprit. By understanding the insecurity cycle, including how insecurity is aroused and how it progresses, many couples who are now stuck may find a way out. Others, by being vigilant, may be able to avoid the worst pitfalls that insecurity can create.

9

Mix and Match: Tough Heart and Tender Heart Together

Every one knows Plato's theory about marriage. He taught that men and women were hemispheres, so to speak, of an original sphere; that ill-assorted marriages were the result of the wrong hemispheres getting together; that, if the true halves met, the man became complete, and the consequence was the "happy-ever-after" of childhood's stories. There is much truth in this doctrine, that for every man there is one woman somewhere in the world, and for every woman one man. They seldom meet in time. If they did, what would become of the sensational novelists?

The above passage appears in a book about marriage that was published in 1886. Written anonymously, *How to be Happy Though Married,* as it was humorously titled, is one of the earliest marriage manuals that I've been able to find. By expressing pessimism about Plato's idea about finding our soul mates and living happily ever after ("They seldom meet in time"), the author takes a fairly pragmatic as opposed to a romantic view of couplehood. He (or she) goes on to offer the following words of advice:

We expect too much from life in general, and from married life in particular. When castle-building before marriage we imagine a condition never experienced on this side of heaven; and when real life comes with its troubles and cares, the tower of romance falls with a crash, leaving us in the mud-hut of every-day reality. Better to enter the marriage state in the frame of mind of that company of American settlers, who, in naming their new town, called it Dictionary, "because," as they said, "that's the only place where peace, prosperity, and happiness are always to be found."

After nearly twenty years of counseling couples I've learned that people make commitments and get married for all kinds of reasons. Certainly every couple I've met made the decision to be together in the belief that life together would somehow be better than a life spent alone. We each have our hopes and expectations for what a committed relationship will do for us. Some people have extremely high expectations: they seek that *one* perfect mate, the *one* perfect match that Plato holds out as an ideal—our fated soul mate. These are people who build castles in the sky. Often they do not expect to have to work on making a relationship work; and they are surprised and dismayed when their high expectations are disappointed. After all, doesn't Plato's ideal imply that eternal bliss would follow the perfect mating? Very often these people lose heart easily and become depressed when things don't go as smoothly as they expected. They give up and leave, rather than looking for ways that things could get better if only they and their partner were willing to change.

Others (probably the majority) enter marriage more like the American settlers did when they started their new town. They hope that marriage will improve their lives, and perhaps even that it will help to complete them in ways; but in their hearts they know from the outset that there is no perfect match. They hope for the best, but they accept the idea that they may have to change, may have to sacrifice, and may have to simply accept some differences in the interest of long-term harmony.

Then there are those who, despite going into a relationship with their eyes wide open—not expecting eternal bliss and willing to work on a relationship—nevertheless come to conclude after a while that they have been deliberately deceived and abused. For them, it can be hard to not give in to bitterness. Their resentment over being used or abused can stand in the way of their willingness to accept differences or to change the way they relate to their partner. Or they may conclude that the situation cannot be improved despite their best efforts to change themselves and their expectations. They may conclude that the situation is simply hopeless, in which case the only sane thing to do is to leave.

The above passages were not written at a time when this last alternative—divorce—was an acceptable option for the unhappily married. For that reason this same book contains much advice on ways to cope with "a bad matrimonial bargain," none of which even mention divorce. Things have changed a great deal since 1886. Today about half of all marriages end in divorce. Indeed, there are some couples I've known who I thought were much better off divorcing, despite the trauma and chaos that divorce can create.

This chapter, though, is not for them. This chapter is for those couples who, after being together for a while, find that their temperaments are not the perfect match that Plato wrote about. But at the same time, their relationship is not so bad that they've concluded divorce is their only reasonable option. In other words, it is for all those couples who find that they are *mismatched* in some ways but who have hope that things can be improved. Most important, it is for those couples who still firmly feel that they love each other and who are open to the idea of doing some work on their relationship in order to make things better.

What do we have to change in order to make a relationship better? It goes without saying that sometimes it's our own behavior that needs to change. We may need to respond to our partners in a different way in the interests of harmony. We may need, for example, to respect differences in outlook, tastes, interests, or preferences, becoming more tolerant in one or more of these areas. Or we may need to be more considerate.

Sometimes, though, we must look deeper. Sometimes it is not just our behavior that we must consider changing, but the *expectations* that drive our behavior. The fact is that expectations are powerful determinants of human behavior. By setting our expectations unrealistically high, we set ourselves up for disappointment, anger, and self-pity. On the other hand, if we set them too low, we may not get enough of our needs met and may end up feeling depressed, and again find ourselves sinking into useless self-pity.

As an example of the reality of how important expectations are, consider the implications for relationships of the two different ways of looking at them just described. What are the long-term chances, do you think, of the following two people being happy?

✓ a person who holds on to the Platonic view, waits for their soul mate to appear, and then expects to live happily ever after
✓ a person who believes that "peace, prosperity, and happiness" can only always be found in a dictionary, so you might as well not expect these things in everyday life

In my experience, it is the second type of person who is the better bet by far for having a good relationship over the long run.

There are many ways in which couples can be mismatched. Interpersonal sensitivity is one important dimension on which a couple's dispositions may differ significantly, and such differences can play a decisive role in whether a relationship grows and succeeds or withers and fails. It isn't an exaggeration to say that differences in interpersonal sensitivity—when a tender heart gets together with a tough heart—can make or break a relationship. The most dangerous situation is when a couple is unaware of a significant difference between them, and also unaware of what they can do to compensate for it.

Couples who differ significantly in how interpersonally sensitive they are will almost always find this difference becoming a factor in their relationship sooner or later. In many cases these differences in temperament will eventually become a source of irritation, if not a source of outright conflict. Unfortunately, most couples will not understand exactly what the problem is. Typically, the tenderhearted partner will feel misunderstood, when the real issue is that they and their tough-hearted partner are simply seeing the world through different lenses. What they'd like, of course, is for their partner to see the world the same way that they do, and to react to it emotionally the same way they do. They usually aren't consciously aware of this, though. Instead, the tenderhearted person may think of their more tough-hearted mate as callous or hardheaded. Sometimes they will see this as something that their partner is doing purposefully: that if they *wanted to,* they could see things and react to them the same way that the more sensitive person does. Over time they can build up stores of resentment over this.

And what does the tough-hearted partner want? In a way, the same thing: they'd also like their partner to see the world the same way they see it. They can be frustrated by a partner whom they see as too soft-headed, too much of a soft touch, too emotional, or not rational enough. They may wish that their partner were less sensitive, more thick-skinned. Without some insight into the reasons for the differences between them and their tenderhearted partners, tough-hearted people run the risk of thinking that the tenderhearted are simply weak, just as the tenderhearted are vulnerable to misjudging their tough-hearted partners, thinking them to be heartless or cold. In most cases these are all stereotypes and oversimplifications. Worse, they are negative judgments that erode the mutual respect a relationship requires in order to stand a chance of being mutually satisfying over the long run.

LIVING WITH A MISMATCH: UNDERSTANDING DIFFERENCES

If two people with different temperaments want to keep the differences between them from undermining their relationship, it is critical that they understand and respect those differences. Understanding and respect, however, are not necessarily the same thing, so let's begin with understanding.

Here are thumbnail descriptions of tenderhearted versus tough-hearted people. After reading them, think about which one describes you and your partner best.

IN PRAISE OF TENDERHEARTED PARTNERS

Tenderhearted people are *empathic.* They not only experience their own emotions deeply but also identify with other people's feelings and can feel them almost as if they were their own. Emotionally speaking, they find it easy to put themselves into another person's shoes, to understand the other person's point of view, and to empathize with what they are feeling. This combination of being in touch with their own feelings and emotional reactions and being able to identify with others' emotional experiences makes the emotional life of tenderhearted people rich and complex.

In casting judgment on their own and other people's behavior, tenderhearted people rely not only on strict rules of right and wrong but also on circumstances. They're inclined to consider extenuating circumstances when deciding whether a particular act is acceptable, as well as what punishment is appropriate for a particular transgression. You could say that the tenderhearted person makes a lot of *subjective* judgments, that they're naturally inclined to put themselves in the other person's shoes when making a moral judgment. The tenderhearted person sees many shades of gray when it comes to deciding on right versus wrong, and on what punishment fits the crime. When they themselves do something that they decide is wrong, especially if what they do results in someone else being hurt, the tenderhearted person will feel a great deal of *guilt*. That's because they will empathize with the other person's injured feelings.

The tenderhearted person is also someone who forms strong *attachments*. They become attached to people, places, and things. Their pets become like family, and they hold on to many sentimental possessions. These are people who keep the same friends for a long time, who are often described as sentimental, and who, if they can, will make their workplace into a home away from home. Because of their tendency to get attached to things in their physical and social environment, tenderhearted people are influenced by it. As a rule they don't like change, especially if that change means having to break ties. In this sense you could say that tenderhearted people are somewhat less *adaptable*.

Finally, because they identify with others' feelings, tenderhearted people prefer to avoid confrontations, particularly angry or hostile ones that arouse anxiety in others. In dealing with conflict they prefer to seek *compromise,* and in general they are more drawn to *cooperation* than to competition. If they do get into competitive situations, they prefer activities that are more friendly and less cutthroat.

IN PRAISE OF TOUGH-HEARTED PARTNERS

In many ways tough-hearted people represent the complement of their tenderhearted counterparts. This does not mean, however, that one is inferior to the other. Tough-hearted people tend to be more emotionally *detached* from others. They may be in touch with their own needs, desires, and feelings. They can feel a full range of emotions, from happiness to sorrow. But they don't necessarily empathize as much with *others'* feelings as much as tenderhearted people do. They are also less prone to becoming strongly attached to people, places, and things than tenderhearted people are. As a result, they are less influenced emotionally by their environment, and changes that involve breaking connections to people, places, and things are less stressful for the tough-hearted person than they are for the tenderhearted. Some might say that tough-hearted are therefore more adaptable when it comes to change.

As for making judgments about what is right versus wrong behavior, tough-hearted people rely more on *objective* rules than on the circumstances. For them, extenuating circumstances are less important than what the rules are. And if they themselves break a rule, they will feel *remorse* for having done something wrong, more than guilt over hurting someone else.

Tough-hearted people are much more comfortable with conflict, confrontation, and competition than tenderhearted people are. The tough-hearted are more likely to play to win, even if winning means that someone else's feelings will get hurt.

The table on page 162 summarizes the differences between those with tenderhearted and those with tough-hearted temperaments.

As you read the descriptions and look through the table, on which side do you think your own temperament falls? Keep in mind that people are not necessarily either totally tenderhearted or totally tough-hearted. It's quite possible that you may identify with some qualities in both columns, which would mean that your own temperament probably lies somewhere in between the two extremes of very tenderhearted and very tough-hearted. On the other hand, you may identify very much with the qualities on one side or the other of the table, and with one of the two descriptions.

TENDERHEARTED	TOUGH-HEARTED
Empathic: identifies with others' feelings.	Detached: mostly in touch with own feelings.
Subjective: judges right versus wrong behavior based on a consideration of the circumstances as much as on the rules.	Objective: judges right versus wrong mostly on the basis of set rules.
Feels guilt if they do something that hurts someone else.	Feels remorse if they break a rule.
Forms strong attachments to people, places, and things.	Less attached to people, places, and things.
Dislikes change that involves breaking attachments.	Adaptable to change.
Dislikes confrontation, prefers cooperation and collaboration over competition.	Comfortable with confrontation; plays to win.

You may also see your partner's temperament described very accurately in one way or the other.

CELEBRATING DIFFERENCES

Insight is half the answer to making a relationship between two people with very different temperaments work. Recognizing differences, however, is not enough. It also takes respect. Couples who have different temperaments and personalities can react to those differences in one of two ways: they can either resent and disrespect them or they can celebrate them.

A colleague of mine who has worked with couples for as many years as I have has a theory of why couples have conflict. We begin a relationship, he argues, because we are attracted to some qualities in another person that we would like to possess. We see them as our *complement;* and secretly we believe that a relationship with that person will make us complete. For example, a serious person may be attracted to someone who takes a lighthearted approach to life; a frugal person may be drawn to someone who has a carefree attitude about money; a sexually repressed individual may be attracted to someone who is sexually adventurous. In order for this process to work, it must be reciprocal. In other words, the sexually adventurous partner must want to balance their sexuality with some restraint. The carefree spender must want, at least in part, to become more frugal. If this kind of *reciprocity* exists between two people who are drawn to each other, it can become the basis for forming a relationship. It's a little like Plato's theory, but with a psychological twist.

At first, these two people share a mutual attraction based on their *complementarity*. Over time, however, the very differences that drew the couple together in the first place begin to become a source of irritation, and eventually of conflict. This is where respect (or lack thereof) comes into play.

Resentment begins to creep into a relationship as the very qualities that brought us together to begin with, and that we may once have liked and respected (or at the very least tolerated), become the qualities we most dislike about each other. At that point alienation begins to set in, and affection and intimacy inevitably suffer.

This process may not apply to every couple, and it may not be the only reason why couples have conflict. I've seen many couples, though, for whom this description fits the bill. Their problems as a couple begin as soon as attraction begins giving way to frustration. At that point one or both of them begin resenting rather than appreciating the differences between them. Instead of wanting to be more like their partner, as they did at the start of their relationship, they start wanting their partner to become more like them.

If any couple was an example of opposites attracting and then having that attraction work against them, David and Lisa were it. As far as I could tell they were complementary in just about every way imaginable. He was blond, with blue eyes and a husky build; she had dark, almost black hair, delicate features, and a slight frame. He was intellectual and extremely articulate; she was emotional and often had to struggle to put her feelings into words. He was self-controlled; she was spontaneous. He was the epitome of social graciousness; she had a reputation for being outspoken, even at the risk of putting someone off. He was restrained; she was not. Lisa was a generous, sensitive, affectionate, and empathic person. David was uncomfortable with public displays of affection, prided himself on being hardheaded, and had a reputation among his friends for being cheap.

David and Lisa were attracted to each other precisely because they each had qualities that fulfilled a need in the other and because they each represented something that the other, at least partly, wanted to be. David found Lisa exciting and funny. He was touched by her gentleness, impressed with her generosity (her willingness to give and not hold back), and charmed by her wit. Though he found it hard to initiate affection, he soaked it up from her. Whereas he was socially uncomfortable, self-conscious, and tentative, she brought spontaneity and feeling to his life. Not to mention good sex. David's previous two long-term relationships had fizzled out, according to him, out of sheer boredom. He knew from the start that that would never happen with Lisa.

When Lisa met David she was impressed by what she perceived to be his stability, maturity, consideration, and intelligence. She described the history of her previous relationships as "a string of not-so-nice, not-too-bright guys," each of whom had turned out in the end to be near-exact replicas of the philandering, substance-abusing stepfather she'd grown up with. She'd had her fill, she said, of irresponsible, adolescent men. She wanted someone grown-up. David, with his reserved demeanor, his careful manners, and his conservative lifestyle, struck her as exactly what she needed in her life.

For about a year David and Lisa were extremely happy together. If anyone had asked them, they each would have said that they'd found their soul mate. Slowly, however, that began to change. The first sign was that David became less willing to socialize with Lisa's friends, even though he'd appeared to have a good time with them before.

Gradually, their social life pretty much dried up. When they did go out with others, despite the fact that David offered no complaints, Lisa sensed that he was becoming more and more uncomfortable with Lisa's outgoing, uninhibited, and sometimes loud friends. When she asked him what was wrong, though, he said, "Nothing."

At home, David started to tease Lisa about how she was so generous with charities, and though he insisted he was only joking, she sensed a definite edge in his voice. Then, when he came home to find that a cat had shown up at the back door and taken up temporary residence, he threw a little tantrum. He got upset even though Lisa made it perfectly clear that she would take full responsibility for the animal, even if she decided to keep it. It was around this same time, David later admitted, that he had begun to see Lisa as someone who was too soft, not tough enough, and something of a spendthrift as well. In other words, he was beginning to show the first signs of resenting, rather than appreciating, the differences in his and Lisa's personalities.

The disenchantment that set into this relationship was by no means a one-way street. Lisa, too, began to feel it. For one thing, she started feeling fenced in by David. "I began to get the sense that he thought I was immature or something. I distinctly remember thinking: 'He wants me to be more serious and reserved, like him.' He used to say that he liked it that I was uninhibited; but after a while, he stopped saying that. That was when I started to see him as stiff."

Lisa began to resent David's frugality, and found his reserved manner increasingly irritating. She was the first to allow her growing disenchantment to erupt into open conflict, reacting with anger to her perception of David's growing disapproval of her and her friends. Being the more sensitive, emotional one in the relationship, it made sense that she would be the first to give a voice to her feelings and bring the tension between them into the open.

David denied Lisa's accusations, though he did admit under pressure from her that he'd been feeling unhappy. When Lisa further pressured him, to go with her to a counselor—confronting him with her feeling that their relationship was slipping away—he reluctantly agreed to go, but only if she agreed to pay.

***

The first step that couples like David and Lisa must take if they hope to salvage their relationship is to recognize the nature of the differences between them. When David and Lisa came into counseling, it took only a single session for us to accomplish that much. They were already aware of the fact that they were different, and even that they'd been attracted to each other because of those differences. They were less aware, though, that the qualities they were drawn to represented qualities they felt were lacking in themselves. They were qualities that they *envied* to a degree. In the time they'd been together, neither had consciously acknowledged this fact. After I pointed out how this seemed to be true, both were able to see it. That insight alone led them both to feel some relief.

The second step was more difficult. That step is for couples whose personalities are complements of each other to come to the point where they appreciate and respect their differences, rather than resenting or pathologizing them. It means learning to accept differences, rather than wishing the other partner were more like oneself. Ironically, these differences are often the ones that draw a couple together to begin with. This is the reason, as my friend and colleague pointed out, why opposites sometimes attract: they each possess some qualities that the other would like to have.

Taking this second step was not as easy for either David or Lisa to do, partly because the differences between them were so great. David had been the man he was—intellectual, frugal, emotionally reserved—all his life, just as Lisa had always been the woman she was, emotional, generous, uninhibited. Even though they both held some envy for the way the other person was, it was not going to be easy for either of them to change their own basic personalities, if they could change them at all.

Since neither David nor Lisa was going to become a different person, their choices, I told them, were either to learn to appreciate their differences or to split. I asked them, though, to consider that a relationship is, in a sense, something greater than either of its parts. A relationship has a life and a personality of its own—one that both partners contribute to. I then asked them to tell me how their relationship was something greater than either one of them individually.

Both David and Lisa had to admit that, as much as they had come to resent the way the other one was, as a *couple* they were much more complete, and more diverse, than either of them was alone. Lisa said that as much as she was uncomfortable with David's reserve and frugality, she thought he had good judgment when it came to people and money. David responded with a bit of a confession: he'd come to feel uncomfortable about the way Lisa was, he said, because *he* would be uncomfortable or embarrassed if *he* acted that way.

David's little admission proved to be the breakthrough that this relationship needed. After listening to what David had to say, I asked Lisa to say something about her discomfort with David. She replied that she felt she could accept—even appreciate—the way he was as compared to her, if only he would do the same. It was mostly her sense of his disapproval, she explained, that made her want to rebel. "When I sense that he wants me to be different, more like *him*—*that* makes me want to be even more like *me*," she said.

This relationship, which at first seemed all but lost, not only was saved but actually entered a period of new growth. Recognizing that the sum is greater than any of its individual parts—that as a *couple* Lisa and David had a life that was richer than what either of them alone could achieve—drew them together again, this time even more strongly than before. Each began to see themselves as part of a larger, better, more promising whole. Rather than feel uncomfortable about their differences, they began to feel proud of them. They started socializing again, only now David found himself laughing again about Lisa's uninhibited nature. And she found herself appreciating David's restraint. "He helps me get my feet back down to earth now and then," she joked. David laughed. "And she helps me lighten up!"

* * *

The differences between us can become sore points. They can tear us apart. Alternatively, our differences can represent opportunities for us to extend ourselves. A relationship does have a life of its own. It has a personality of its own, too, one that is greater than the sum of the individual personalities that make it up. In order for a tenderhearted person and a tough-hearted one to get the most out of their relationship, they need to recognize these truths. Otherwise they may find themselves pulling apart, diminishing their relationship, instead of pulling together and expanding it.

Key questions to ask yourself, if you find yourself struggling with differences between yourself and your partner, are listed below. Answer each of these questions for yourself. Better yet, use them as the basis for a dialogue between you.

* To what extent do you think that you and your partner were originally attracted to each other on the basis of *complementarity;* in other words, on the basis of the *differences* between you?

* What qualities in your partner were you most attracted to at first?

* Which of these qualities in your partner did you think would add to the quality of a life together?

* Do you think you may have ever secretly wished you could be more like your partner? In what ways?

* Is sensitivity one way in which you and your partner differ? Which one of you is the more tenderhearted one? Which one of you is more tough-hearted?

* At some point in your relationship, did the differences between you and your partner stop being something appealing and start instead to become a source of irritation?

* In what ways did you start wishing that, instead of being different, your partner were more like you?

* Have you ever felt that either you or your partner had lost respect for the ways in which the two of you are different?

Through answering (or better yet, discussing) the above questions, you can gain some insights into what drew you and your partner together initially. These questions can give you some insight into the ways in which you thought you were deficient—ways you wished you were more like the person you were attracted to. It can also help to pinpoint the source of any disenchantment or conflict that may have started creeping into your relationship.

The next step is to answer the following questions. Again, a discussion with your partner can prove much more productive than simply answering these questions alone.

* Do you still resent the differences between you and your partner? In other words, do you still want your partner to be less like themselves, more like you?

* Are there any differences between you and your partner that, in your opinion, could make your *relationship* stronger, more rounded and complete? In other words, is there anything you could accomplish together that neither of you could accomplish alone?

* In what specific ways do the differences between you and your partner make life together a richer experience than what either of you would experience alone?

* Can you put your appreciation for the differences between you and your partner into words? Specifically, if you are a tenderhearted/tough-hearted pair, in what ways do each of your temperaments contribute to your relationship? In what situations does each temperament have its advantages?

* Can you name some examples of how your relationship brings out the best in you?

If differences between you and your partner, for example in how sensitive you are, have become a source of irritation or conflict, the first thing you need to do is to decide whether those differences are simply too big for you to be able to work together successfully. Sometimes this may be the case, but chances are it isn't. More often, couples struggle blindly with their differences, being unable to name or understand them, and frustrated as to how to combine them so as to make the relationship as a whole stronger than either of its two parts alone. This was certainly true for Lisa and David. Although they had both been aware that their attraction had been based in part on their being opposites, they did not have a clear understanding of some of those differences, particularly the different ways they responded emotionally to the world. They were only dimly aware of how what had started as attraction had turned into irritation.

Being attracted to someone who complements us seems to be a natural human tendency. Perhaps Plato was right in one way: we each seek to complete ourselves. What couples like David and Lisa must appreciate, though, is that we as individuals can alter our personalities only so much. And we may not be able to change our innate temperaments very much at all. So the goal then becomes to look beyond ourselves as individuals. We need to recognize the *personality* of each relationship we form. We must be willing to surrender ourselves—our individual egos—to some extent to that greater whole, in order for it to grow. This means finding the humility to admit that we cannot be self-sufficient. It means recognizing and getting comfortable with the idea that we can realize more fulfillment together than we can alone. As the example of David and Lisa shows, this is entirely possible to do.

10

The Road Back: From Insecurity to Confidence

Okay, so you admit it: you *are* a little insecure. Maybe even more than a little. Now, you ask, what can you do about it?

Sensitivity does not have to lead to insecurity. It is not inevitable— a fate awaiting every sensitive soul that is born. On the contrary, sensitive children who are raised by parents who recognize and nurture their sensitivity and provide a secure network of attachments for their child will raise children who are sensitive but secure. Unfortunately, as many of the examples described in this book show, not all sensitive people are so fortunate. The natural question that many of these people have is this: is it possible for insecure men and women to shed that insecurity and to discover the sensitivity they were born with, without the added burden of insecurity? These people, who have suffered from insecurity and still do, want to know what they can do to recover their sensitivity.

Although the temperaments we are born with, including how interpersonally sensitive we are, are probably not very changeable, insecurity *is* something that a person can work to overcome. That's because while sensitivity is something we are born with and will have forever, insecurity is learned. And what can be learned can be *un*learned.

By learning to reduce their insecurity, insecure people can rediscover their basic sensitivity. They can learn to enjoy the benefits of being a person who is naturally empathic, who forms attachments, and who enjoys a depth of feeling. They can learn to experience this without the burden of anxiety and self-doubt that insecurity brings with it.

Insecure people can help to improve their situations in several ways. They can begin by learning to adjust their *expectations*. Next, they can work through the buried *emotions* that were associated with their becoming insecure in the first place. Finally, they can learn to engage in *constructive conflict*. We can think of each of these as different *pathways* from insecurity to sensitivity. Let's look at each one.

STEP 1: CHANGING EXPECTATIONS

Insecure people often turn their relationships into self-fulfilling prophecies. They are eternally vigilant for signs of abandonment, abuse, or rejection. They tend to approach life with a distrustful attitude. Instead of being optimistic—believing that people are essentially trustworthy, and then waiting for evidence to the contrary before they conclude otherwise—they take a pessimistic approach: they assume that others are *not* trustworthy and look for evidence to support their bias. Here is an example.

* * *

Holly described her husband, Ben, as possessive and jealous. He was both of these things; and of course, he was also insecure. Throughout his youth he'd been the victim of his father's mean and unpredictable temper. Ben was a "Junior," and the elder Ben, who'd always enjoyed a fight and who had a rough-and-tumble lifestyle, regarded his son as soft. He'd challenge Ben Junior to do something reckless, like walk the edge of a nearby railroad trestle as though it were a tightrope. Whenever Ben would balk at one of these challenges (as he often did), his father would call him a sissy, and sometimes even slapped him in rebuke.

His father also tried to goad Ben into being a fighter, like him. He was forever advising him, for example, to beat up on kids at school if they gave him a hard time. Here, too, Ben disappointed his father. He'd ignore the advice, only to be subjected to more ridicule.

Ben's father was physically and verbally abusive of Ben's mother, and he frequently expressed the same distrustful sentiments toward her that Ben eventually came to act out in his relationships. "People are no good" was a comment that Ben had heard his father make more times than he could count. He said it in response to anything and everything. Ben Senior would rant on and on all the time about how people could not be trusted. "Women in particular," he'd say, without ever explaining himself. Rarely did a meal go by that Ben's father would not put down his own wife, his son, someone he worked with, or another family member at least once. He was always finding fault, and outrightly called people cheats, liars, and thieves, as much to their faces as behind their backs. Given his immersion in these attitudes, plus his own abuse, it was no surprise to me that Ben turned out to be insecure.

By the time he was a young adult, Ben had established a pattern in his relationships that made them into self-fulfilling prophecies. It would start out with him choosing a girl who most people would judge to be pleasant, perhaps a little shy, but definitely sensitive and nurturing. He'd pursue this girl with vigor, flattering her and heaping attention on her. He'd buy her little gifts, pass her notes, leave her cards. By his actions he would leave no doubt in the girl's mind that he'd fallen absolutely head over heels for her.

Every one of Ben's girlfriends was initially drawn to him in part because of the attention he paid them and the way he treated them. It wasn't long, however, before they each began to feel some discomfort in the relationship. The source of their discomfort was always the same: they quickly began to feel smothered by Ben. It would start with his being possessive. He'd want to be with them all the time—and I mean *all* the time. His demands for attention escalated quickly, and soon became obnoxious. His neediness took up so much of a girl's time that Ben had found himself confronted more than once by an irritated parent and told fairly directly to back off.

Ben also quickly became distrustful and jealous of each of his girl-friends. They would find themselves being questioned about who they had been talking to, who they had been spending time with, and why. If they were late—even a few minutes late—for a meeting with him, or if they couldn't see him because of another commitment, they were liable to be grilled with hostile, accusing questions: "You're dating that guy from history class, right? You have a better time with your girlfriends than you do with me, right?"

The final stage in Ben's relationships was marked by anger. His behavior toward his girlfriends would make them angry; but he in turn would also inevitably feel betrayed and angry as well. Regardless of how nice they were, many of his girlfriends ended up doing the very things he'd been accusing them of so relentlessly: going out on him, preferring to be with friends rather than with him, lying to him about where they'd been or why they couldn't see him. I felt certain that at least some of them must have acted this way in retaliation. It wasn't hard to imagine how stifled and how resentful they must have felt at times. People do not like to be controlled, and no one likes to be distrusted when there is no good reason for it. In his insecurity, however, Ben subjected his girlfriends to both. He tried to control their every move, and in word and deed he let them know that he didn't trust them.

Ben had created and suffered his own self-fulfilling prophecies many times over before he ever met Holly. By then he was in his early thirties. He had his own business, had recently bought a house, and was having fun shopping for antiques. In many ways it was the best time of his life, and he met Holly when he was riding the crest of this wave of good fortune. She, meanwhile, was in her late twenties, a beauty with long auburn hair, a freckled complexion, and a broad, engaging smile. She was by nature happy, and *not* an insecure person. She was also an exceptionally nurturing woman, and unlike those who had come (and gone) before her, she was somehow able to tolerate Ben's possessiveness and insulate herself from his jealousy as their relationship moved out of the courtship stage and Ben's insecurity, as it inevitably did, began to rear its ugly head. She told me that she thought she could see beyond his insecurity to the sensitive soul beneath it. "I firmly believed in the Ben I fell in love with," she said, "not the Ben who started coming out."

For two years after marrying Ben, Holly endured his full-blown insecurity. She put up with his ceaseless demands for attention, his brooding when he didn't get enough of it, his controlling ways, and his accusations when he imagined her being unfaithful or rejecting him in some way. She truly loved him a great deal, and she continued to believe in his basic sensitivity and his capacity for love. She also sensed the woundedness that drove his intense insecurity; but finally she, too, had enough. The last straw came when she innocently told Ben one evening that her boss had brought her flowers for National Secretary's Day. "Roses," she'd said, a smile on her face. "He said I've just done such a good job that he only wished they could be *gold-plated* roses!" She'd put them, she said, on the table in the living room, because they looked so nice in there.

Ben exploded. He accused Holly of having an affair with her boss. Then he ran into the living room, snatched up the vase of roses, and threw it against the wall. It bounced off, smashing into a picture of Holly's parents that sat on a table, then hit the floor and shattered.

Ben cursed, called Holly vile names, and stormed out of the house. He didn't return until long after she'd gone to bed. The next day she asked him to go to counseling with her. He refused. She asked him several times again over the next several weeks. Things didn't get any better between them; in fact, he seemed to get more irritable and critical than ever.

When she decided to separate, Holly left Ben a note, which he found when he got home from work one Friday night. In it she explained that she'd been fearful of what he might do if she confronted him face-to-face with her decision. She wrote that she was moving out for a while. She wasn't asking for a legal separation or a divorce; but she did ask Ben not to try to contact her until she contacted him. She explained the reasons for her decision. Basically, it was Ben's insecurity: his jealousy and possessiveness, his tendency to brood until she gave him the attention he craved, and finally, his anger. She'd hoped that these would all subside over time as he came to realize how much she loved him. She'd told herself that he was just immature and that he would grow. But reluctantly, she said, she'd finally come to the conclusion that no matter what she did, Ben would never be able to believe in his heart that she loved him. She'd also come to the conclusion that whatever Ben's problem was, he wouldn't just outgrow it.

* * *

Ben's jealousy, anger, and possessiveness were all signs of his insecurity. More specifically, these destructive behaviors were driven by his unconscious and unrealistic expectations for relationships. From the time he was an adolescent, Ben's behavior in relationships reflected these expectations, which included:

✓ It is reasonable to expect constant attention.
✓ It is reasonable to expect continual approval from our partners.
✓ It is reasonable to expect that our partners will have no interests or commitments other than ourselves.
✓ It is reasonable to expect that someone who loves us will never say or do anything to hurt our feelings.
✓ It is reasonable to expect that someone who loves us will never get angry at us.

When insecure people read statements like the above, their first reaction is often to deny that they have such expectations. That's what Ben did. "I don't believe any of those things," he protested. However, when you ask their partners, they will tell you that insecure people definitely *act* as if they held such expectations. This was true beyond a doubt for Ben's actions, as attested to by Holly when she read this same list. "Yes," she said simply, "this is Ben, all right."

What accounts for the discrepancy between what insecure people say they believe and the way they act and what others perceive about them? The answer is that these expectations are *unconscious*. They may seem unreasonable on their face when read by an insecure adult; but it is the insecure *child* within that adult who is most often holding these expectations.

The more insecure a person is—and Ben was very insecure—the more their actions appear to be guided by unrealistic expectations. The fact that they are not consciously aware of these expectations only attests to the fact that the roots of insecurity often lie deep in the past, in experiences that insecure men and women themselves may not have thought about for many years.

One side effect that is directly attributable to irrational expectations like the above is the distrust and sense of betrayal that insecure people are so quick to feel, plus the frustration, and sometimes anger, that gets generated in those who are in relationships with them. Insecure people are chronically feeling let down by others; yet what they fail to realize is that their standards are so unrealistically high that it's inevitable that they will feel let down. Like Ben, they often look for proof that others can't be counted on, then justify their distrust when they find that proof. But they also create that proof by setting the bar so high that no one could consistently jump over it. This was an analogy that Holly identified with: "I've always felt like I had to jump hurdles for Ben, to prove to him that I love him. I suppose I did this willingly at first, because I knew in my heart that he had a wounded soul. The problem, though, was that every time I made it over a hurdle, Ben just came right back with another, higher one. I really thought they'd get lower, and eventually go away. But I was wrong."

I asked Holly how she reacted to that—to having to prove her love. "It's extremely frustrating," she replied. "It makes me feel that I'm bound to fail, sooner or later, in Ben's eyes, because sooner or later I'll fail one of his tests. And to tell the truth, it also makes me angry. I know I love him, and I don't like being doubted. I don't do that to him. I don't constantly ask him to prove that *he* loves *me*."

* * *

If Ben was to have any chance of salvaging his relationship with Holly, I told him, he would have to begin by examining the expectations he had for relationships, and then *changing* them. His new expectations would need to look more like the following:

✓ It is reasonable to expect attention in relationships, but it is *not* reasonable to expect constant attention. In general, we should be giving others about as much attention as we expect to get in return.

✓ It is reasonable for us to expect approval and support from our partners, but *not* constantly, for that would imply that we are perfect, which we most certainly are not.

✓ It is reasonable to expect that our partners *will* have at least some interests or commitments other than ourselves, and that these interests and commitments will take them away from us at times.

✓ It is reasonable to expect that someone who loves us will *sometimes* say or do something that hurts our feelings, since neither we nor they are perfect.

✓ It is reasonable to expect that someone who loves us will *sometimes* get angry at us, for we are not perfect.

If Ben could work on embracing expectations like the above, while at the same time trying to catch himself acting out on unconscious expectations like those listed earlier, I guaranteed him that his life would change profoundly.

In reading through the above, take careful note of the word *perfect,* which appears several times. The unconscious, unrealistic expectations that insecure people hold are based in an unconscious fantasy that there can be such a thing as a perfect relationship: a relationship in which we are constantly approved of, in which we always get what we want and are always the center of attention, and in which we can never do wrong. What all of these expectations have in common is that they are very *childlike.* They are the wishful thinking of a child. If you think about it, this makes sense, since the roots of insecurity usually lie in our childhood experiences. In a way, insecure people are simply trying to make up, in their adult relationships, for wounds that were suffered early in their lives. The earlier the wounds and the deeper they run, the more the insecure person has to *compensate* for, and the more unrealistic their expectations can be. Ben definitely had deep wounds, and he'd suffered them early in life. So his expectations for relationships were that much more unrealistic than they might be for a less insecure person.

Ben's anger, like the anger of all insecure people, comes from deep inside. It is an anger that may have been buried for countless years, along with the pain that children experience when their connection to someone they love and are attached to is broken, be it by physical separation, neglect, rejection, or abuse. Back when the trauma originally occurred, the child may have appeared to get over it, but in fact their grief merely went underground, where it will remain until it is recognized for what it is, and dealt with rather than ignored. Although the pain and anger are buried, they are not inactive. Rather, they are more like the tectonic plates that lie beneath the surface of our planet: we are not aware of them from where we stand on the surface, but they definitely influence what goes on around us. Insecurity is like that: it lies beneath the surface, influencing the way we see and relate to the world. One of the ways it does this is through the expectations that insecure people have for relationships. The anger of insecure people gets set off when their unrealistic expectations are not met. It would be a mistake, though, to attribute all of an insecure person's anger to what is going on in the moment. Yes, she or he may be feeling frustrated over something that is happening in the moment; but the anger that comes out of them flows from a deeper well than that. It is out of proportion to what is going on in the moment. That is what makes it so potentially destructive. It really is like the earthquake that has its roots in some deep fissure. In insecure people that fissure lies in their souls.

It would be disingenuous to claim that it was easy for Ben (or for any insecure person) to change his expectations—to make them more reasonable. However, it is essential that they do this if insecure men and women hope to heal their insecurity and rediscover the sensitivity that lies beneath it. It is also true that this process leads to deep and lasting changes in an insecure person's self-concept and in their relationships. The process starts when the insecure person recognizes that the way they act in relationships reflects some unrealistic expectations on their part. Of course, if it is true that they are being abused in a relationship now, then that's a different story. In that case they need to stand up for themselves. But what we are talking about here is not that circumstance, but rather Ben's circumstance. He was not being abused at all by Holly, who had a great capacity for love, which was being burned out by Ben's insecurity. Many insecure persons create self-fulfilling prophecies the same way Ben was doing with Holly and had done with others before.

Predictably, Ben's first reaction to my suggestion that he had unrealistic expectations for a relationship—expectations so unrealistic that he was virtually certain to be disappointed—was to deny it and argue with me. To his credit, though, Ben was able to step back and look at himself and his personality with a critical, objective perspective and make some decisions about ways he needed to change. This in turn opened the door to change in his relationship with Holly.

***

To follow in Ben's footsteps, answer the following questions about your behavior and your expectation for relationships:

* Has anyone ever told you that you expect too much in relationships? What were the circumstances, and what was said?

* In the important relationships you've had, have you often felt let down by your partner? How much of this might be due to the fact that you expect too much, rather than that they give too little, and that it's your expectations that cause you to be easily disappointed?

* Are you thin-skinned, quick to have your feelings hurt by something your partner says or does? If so, do you believe that if your partner really loved you, your feelings would never get hurt?

* Has someone close to you ever accused you of wanting them to be perfect? Could there be a kernel of truth in this complaint?

It isn't difficult to see how anyone who held expectations like the above would have problems in their relationships. If this describes you in any way, you can expect to be frequently hurt, disappointed, and angry in your relationships. You will end up resenting your partner, and you may end up feeling sorry for yourself, but doing nothing. The pain you experience will be due mostly to some insecurity that you are carrying around. It will *not* be due to your partner's failings or inadequacies. It is not your partner who needs to change—to get better. It is *you* who need to adjust your expectations if you hope to be happier, and also to make your partner happier. Sooner or later, your unchecked insecurity can and will undermine your relationships.

Learning to adjust expectations is not any easier to do than is recognizing unrealistic expectations in the first place. Like learning to change any behavior, changing expectations takes practice. Ben had to learn to catch himself responding to Holly in an unrealistic way, then to stop and think for a moment about what kind of expectation was driving that reaction. The difficult part was learning to pause in the middle of an emotional reaction and then thinking about what disappointed expectation was responsible for it. His natural tendency was just to let the reaction go, even though that would be destructive. He'd had years and years of practice letting go of anger, but not much practice at all with stopping and thinking about why he was angry. He'd always taken his underlying expectations for granted—in fact, he wasn't even aware of them. So, for him to learn to connect his emotions and actions to some hidden expectations, and then to change those expectations, was no small task.

As complicated as this process of changing expectations may sound, it really isn't. It's actually quite possible to do. The key lies in your willingness to *pause* when you feel angry, disappointed, or frustrated with your partner, and to look for a moment at yourself, not just at your partner, as the cause of your feelings. With some practice Ben was able to do just that. The pathway from insecurity to sensitivity, however, was not without its bumps along the way. There were times when Ben could not put the brakes on his insecurity. These were times when he would lose his temper and say something he would later regret. There were other times, though, when he was able to catch himself before his emotions got out of hand. At those times he discovered that some of the above unrealistic expectations did indeed fit him. And as he saw this, things began to change.

STEP 2: UNLOCKING EMOTIONS

Interesting things begin to happen when a person starts to change his or her expectations. For one, the emotions they were experiencing initially—when their behavior was guided by their unrealistic expectations—often change. For Ben, this meant going from feeling angry a lot of the time to feeling suddenly very sad. Before he started changing his expectations, almost anything that Holly would do (or *not* do) could set him off. Anger was quick to build inside him. He could be critical and angry without ever realizing how it had happened.

Now Ben was learning to pause. Whenever he could catch himself feeling frustrated or irritated, he'd stop and think about the expectations we'd talked about. Often, he admitted, he acted like he really did expect Holly to be perfect. He acted as though he expected her to give him all her attention, all the time. He had practically no tolerance for anything other than himself being a priority in her life. He told me he had no idea where these expectations could have come from. He understood about his childhood abuse, but he'd never made any connection between that and what he expected in his relationships. When I suggested that he could be secretly expecting his relationships to make up for what he'd suffered as child, the connection began to appear.

If unrealistic expectations drive disappointment, frustration, and anger, then what happens when a person begins to examine and drop those expectations? Usually, people feel sad, sometimes extraordinarily sad. This is exactly what happened to Ben. He found himself going from clenched fists to weepy eyes. I told him that this was a normal part of the healing process. Once he let go of expecting Holly to fulfill his every need, he was open to feeling the pain and emptiness he'd kept buried, deep down inside him, since childhood. This was pain that he hadn't allowed himself to experience very much when he'd suffered his abuse, probably because it was more than he could handle at the time. He could recall feeling hurt when his father would hit him, or call him soft or a sissy. And he remembered times when he wished he could be closer to his father, as some of his friends were with their fathers. But as best he could recollect, he'd never experienced the deep, aching pain that he was experiencing now.

It can be frightening to feel the pain and the sadness that can well up in you if you reevaluate and let go of unrealistic expectations. Suddenly, all the frustration and anger that has taken center stage for so long in your life just disappears. What comes in its place is what created the unrealistic expectations in the first place: the disappointment, the pain, the anxiety and loneliness that made you insecure. Sometimes these feelings can be so intense, can come in such a torrent, that people think they might be going crazy.

Dealing with long-buried pain can be especially frightening if you do not have someone in your life who can be there to understand and comfort you. Fortunately for Ben, Holly had chosen to separate but didn't really want to divorce him. First in counseling, and later by themselves, they were able to explore Ben's past and how it had come to play such a decisive role in the way he'd been in relationships all his life. Most importantly for Ben, Holly's love had not yet been destroyed by his insecurity. He was able to unburden himself, and she was able to comfort him; and that comfort and love helped heal his wounds.

As insecurity begins to fade, the sensitive person that lies beneath that insecurity begins to emerge. Ben was indeed a sensitive man, though he hadn't pursued many outlets for his sensitivity since childhood. Instead, he'd tried to live a manly life—one, ironically, that his father would have been proud of, despite the fact that on a conscious level Ben had never expressed anything but resentment toward his dad. Any interests he'd ever had that might be inconsistent with his image of manliness were quickly abandoned. The result was that he didn't think of himself as sensitive at all. Holly, though, expressed again, as she had earlier, her strong belief that at heart Ben was a very sensitive man. She pointed out how nurturing he could be at times, and some of the ways that his sensitivity showed through despite his best efforts to conceal it. "I really wouldn't have married you," she told him in one of our sessions, "if I didn't believe in that big heart and sensitive soul that I know you have."

***

If you want to recover from insecurity, the healing process will begin when you are ready to start reevaluating your expectations for relationships. I advise you not to do this alone, for the very reasons that were so obvious in Ben's case as well as the other cases discussed in this book: you may be unaware of any connection between your behavior and your unconscious expectations. On the other hand, others, especially those who love you, may be very aware of these connections. It would be better, then, to include someone else in your recovery process.

You will very likely discover that, unconsciously, you have harbored some pretty unrealistic expectations. As you begin to let go of these, you may find that the feelings of irritation, resentment, or frustration that you are so familiar with begin to give way to uncomfortable feelings like pain, sorrow, anxiety, or loneliness. These can be frightening feelings, because unlike anger—which is directed at some *external* target that we can blame for making us angry—fear, loneliness, and sorrow are *internal;* they are within us. As a result we can feel helpless over them.

Healing the emotions that underlie insecurity means opening ourselves to others. The only way these emotions can be healed is for us to share them with someone and to be comforted by them. This means we must learn to *trust.* This can be the most difficult challenge that an insecure person has to face. It's easy to be angry; it's much harder to expose our pain. It's easy to be guarded; it's much harder to trust. Be patient with yourself in this process of learning to trust and open up. At the same time, recognize that no one can force you to do these things. It is only you, and you alone, who have the power to open you up, to make you trust.

STEP 3: APPROACHING CONFLICTS AND DIFFERENCES

There is one more bridge that insecure people must cross on their journey from insecurity to sensitivity, and that has to do with conflict. As resentful and angry as insecure people can get, they basically do not like conflict. When faced with a potential conflict in their relationship, insecure people generally do not choose constructive confrontation as a way of dealing with it. Instead, insecure people choose one of two other options: *fight* or *flight*. Holly described this very clearly with Ben. Not that there was a whole lot of conflict in their relationship. On the contrary, Holly was a very patient, forgiving person, who tolerated a lot of Ben's irritability and who could endure much criticism from him before she would react. However, there were those occasions when her own self-respect demanded that she push back.

Besides defending herself at times, there were occasions when Holly had legitimate complaints of her own about Ben. As much as he expected from her, he was far from a perfect husband. Issues naturally came up between them, as they do in any relationship. Holly did not like the fact, for example, that Ben would sometimes make major purchases without talking to her first. But Holly found it very difficult to get Ben to address issues like this.

Like many insecure people, Ben's first response to being confronted, however gently, was to *flee*. Sometimes this meant literally leaving the house. His cue was for Holly to say something like, "Can we talk for a minute?" Ben could tell, he told me, from Holly's tone of voice that she was wanting to confront him about something. As soon as he perceived this he would immediately find some excuse to leave—for example, a chore that couldn't wait and had to be done right then. As Holly described it, "Ben can't get out of the house soon enough when I want to talk about something that's bothering me."

A variation of this flight response is also very common among insecure people, and that is to clam up and refuse to get into a discussion. Insecure people may plead fatigue ("I'm too tired to talk about this now") or illness ("I've got a headache") or stress ("I've got too much on my mind") as ways of putting off a confrontation.

If all else fails, the insecure person may resort to the alternative, which is to *fight*. Because conflict arouses such intense anxiety in them, insecure people typically build up a lot of anger before letting it go. This is what makes the insecure person's anger so dangerous. It usually comes gushing forth from a deep well of resentment. Its intent is defensive—to get the other person to back off. In the process, however, the insecure person's anger can be very destructive. They may lose their temper completely, and say and do things that others would describe as out of character for them.

Insecure people often use anger in a preemptive manner. If an insecure person feels that he will not be able to escape a confrontation, he may choose to strike first—to beat the other person to the punch with a complaint of his own. In this scenario, a partner initiates a conversation with the goal in mind of confronting an insecure person about their behavior, only to discover that they are quickly defending themselves and their own behavior. This, of course, is the goal of the fight response: it gets the insecure person off the hook. It puts the spotlight on the other person instead, and makes them want to back off, which is exactly what the insecure person wants to happen.

Ben had used all of these techniques at various times in order to avoid being confronted by Holly. Like all insecure people, no matter how he might appear on the outside, on the inside his sense of self-esteem was so fragile that the idea of being criticized or confronted was too frightening to deal with. People who must deal with insecure partners or coworkers often find this hard to believe, especially since insecure people can be so good at complaining about or criticizing others. The truth is, though, that part of being thin-skinned is the inability to hear something negative about yourself, or rather, the inability to keep criticism in *perspective*. To the insecure person, whose ego is fragile, any criticism at all can be devastating. It's as though the idea that they may have any faults or flaws at all is absolutely unbearable to them.

One reason why insecure people have such a hard time dealing with criticism and engaging in constructive confrontation probably has to do with wounds that run deep, usually into early childhood, where they have remained buried for a long time. Buried, but not healed. It seems that any kind of interaction that has even a remote connection to rejection or abuse—for example, normal anger or complaints by others—can set off the pain and anger that were associated with the original wounds.

Insecure people need to learn to tolerate their pain long enough to hear out someone else's complaint about them, without fleeing, getting defensive, or retaliating. They are better able to do this once they've made some headway with the other goals described above; that is, with identifying their unconscious, unrealistic expectations for others and working through their buried feelings. Still, learning to approach conflict in a healthy way is not easy for someone who's learned to either flee from it or chase it away.

STEP 4: LISTEN, LEARN, AND COMPROMISE

For those who feel they are ready to approach conflicts and differences, instead of just chasing them away, wishing them away, or running from them, here are some guidelines.

·Listen.

Chances are your initial reaction to any confrontation will be anxiety. Before you give in to this and either run away or attack, take a breath and tell yourself to listen. Hear the other person out without reacting in a defensive way. If necessary, keep telling yourself things like the following:

"Confrontation won't kill me. This person cares about me."

"I don't have to be perfect. It's okay if someone else has a complaint about me."

· Learn.

Before you react, find out exactly what it is that the other person expects of you. Do they want an apology? Would they like you to change your behavior, and if so, how?

· Compromise.

Resist any urge to look at a confrontation as a win-lose proposition. That kind of thinking drives anxiety and makes a fight-or-flight response in you all the more likely. Remember: good relationships don't rely on one partner being the winner and the other being the loser; they rely on both partners being winners through compromise. Once you learn what the other person wants, try to decide whether you can just give it to them. If so, that might solve the problem and make you both happy. It can also make the other person appreciate you. On the other hand, if what the other person is asking strikes you as more than you can give, try compromising. Learn to give in order to get, and you'll soon see just how well a relationship can work.

These simple guidelines can go a long way toward breaking the ice in a relationship that has become frozen as a result of insecurity. Learning to approach conflicts in a healthy way, rather than either running from them or trying to chase them away, builds commitment and strengthens relationships. I said earlier that a relationship has a personality and a life of its own. It is also true that a relationship needs teamwork, compromise, and the capacity to deal with conflict, in order to thrive. If you deprive a relationship of these things, it will eventually wither; but if you nourish a relationship with communication and compromise, it will continue to grow forever.

11

Finding Your Emotional Mate

The challenge of finding a partner who is a good match for you is as much a matter of avoiding those who are definitely *bad* matches as it is of finding a good one. It's best to begin this process of finding your emotional mate by making sure you have a clear understanding of what kind of person *you* are. That means, among other things, taking a personal inventory of what your goals are for a long-term relationship. Are you looking primarily for *companionship*—someone to share experiences with—or do you want a *partner,* in the sense of someone to share financial responsibility, pursue long-term goals, perhaps even have children with? Both are perfectly reasonable goals. Your answers to this question, though, can be crucial to determining what you should be looking for in a potential partner. It's surprising how many people do not really have a good sense of what their goals are before they enter a relationship. Either they haven't taken the time to reflect on this or else they don't want to admit to themselves, for one reason or another, what they really want. Some, for example, think they ought to want a commitment, when it's obvious from their history and what they say that what they really want is a companion.

Equally important is knowing what a potential partner's goals are. Again, a surprising number of people I've known either don't bother to check this out at the beginning of a relationship or else assume that someone they are interested in will change their goals once they get into a relationship. Having incompatible goals will almost certainly become a problem, and very likely a fatal one, for any long-term relationship. As a general rule I have learned to advise the people I counsel to believe what someone tells them, or what someone else's *behavior* tells them, about what they are looking for. In other words, if they say they are looking for companionship, or if their history of relationships over the past several years tells you that, don't try to convince yourself that they are really looking for a commitment. I can't even begin to guess how many broken hearts have been the result of this misjudgment alone.

Avoiding bad matches also means understanding your own personality. This includes having some insight into how interpersonally sensitive you are, as well as how insecure you might be. By this time you should have some sense of yourself in both of these areas. If you've discovered that you are insecure, hopefully you will have taken some initial steps toward conquering that insecurity.

Depending on just how insecure you think you are, finding a good match may need to take a backseat for a while until you have a better handle on your insecurity. That's why I decided to place this chapter here, rather than earlier in the book. By the time you are reading this you will hopefully have gained some insight into yourself and any insecurity you may have, and have tried to do something to reduce it. However, if you find that you continue to get into relationships where you end up feeling used or abused, or where you seem to drive potential partners away, then you may need to take some time to work on yourself before looking for a good relationship.

AVOIDING THE WRONG PERSON

Let's turn our attention now to the issue of how to avoid getting together with the wrong person. Surely one such type to avoid is the *emotional predator,* a person who is born with a very tough-hearted temperament to begin with but who *also* has been abused and intimidated as a child. Insensitivity itself is not enough to create a predator—that requires insensitivity plus abuse.

As adolescents and adults, emotional predators model themselves after their abusers. If their abuser was cruel and sadistic, then that is the way they come to approach relationships themselves. They empathize poorly with others, which is a big reason why it is so easy for them to be cruel—just like the person or persons who were cruel to them. Similarly, their ideas about right versus wrong behavior have a lot to do with what they can get away with, and very little to do with social norms or other people's feelings.

Despite their common core, emotional predators are not all alike on the outside. Some can be very coarse and obvious, but others can be very clever and subtle. It all depends on how intelligent they are and what style of abuse or exploitation they were exposed to when they were growing up. If they were treated coarsely, they will model that way of relating to the world, using bald threats or physical abuse to get their way. On the other hand, if the person who coached them used more subtle techniques, such as manipulation and deceit, then that is what they will come to rely on as well.

Clinically, in order to identify an emotional predator, I rely on a series of signs. You may find these useful as well. In general, the more tough-hearted a person is by nature, the more they themselves have been abused, and the more they were exposed as a child to someone who modeled and encouraged cruelty, the more harmful they will be as adults. Usually, a predatory personality begins to make its appearance by late childhood. Intentional cruelty to others and to animals, an inability to express true remorse or guilt after breaking rules or hurting others, a lack of empathy, and a tendency to alienate peers are early signs of a predatory nature.

The first warning sign that you may be relating with (or *trying* to relate with) an emotional predator is their lack of empathy. They don't feel other people's pain, relate to their grief, or identify with their anxiety, including yours. When you interact with them you get the distinct impression that they don't understand how you feel. It's as though they just can't put themselves into your shoes. They're in touch with their own needs and feelings but they lack compassion for others.

Some sensitive people have a hard time accepting the idea that there are people who lack the capacity for empathy and compassion. It is not only foreign but almost inconceivable to them that other people are not like them. If you are a sensitive type, you may be vulnerable to making this mistake. You may want to reject the idea that someone you are either attracted to or in a relationship with may not be capable of relating to what you feel. Alternatively, you might try convincing yourself that you could help them become more empathic. This could be another big mistake.

A more ominous sign to watch out for is someone who has a history of being deliberately cruel to animals or people and who expresses no remorse or guilt over it. Similarly, someone who seems to enjoy fighting or teasing people to the point of cruelty is someone who should set off alarms in you. Similarly, if they seem to take inordinate pleasure in teasing you even after you've told them to stop, if they seem to find fighting with you exciting, or if they just can't take no for an answer, you'd best beware.

Next, be wary of someone who never takes any personal responsibility for any problems or difficulties they have. Emotional predators are governed by a simple principle: whatever you can get away with is okay. A corollary of this is: whatever you can't get away with is somebody else's fault. They never apologize, at least not sincerely. When they can't get their way, they get mad. Compromise is a difficult concept for them to grasp. They are not just assertive—they are downright aggressive and dominating.

Emotional predators make poor partners regardless of how sensitive you may or may not be. Even tough-hearted people, in other words, are likely to find themselves victimized if they get into a relationship with a predator. Tough-hearted people are more emotionally detached than tenderhearted people, but they are not amoral. They have a good sense of what is right versus wrong, and they use that to govern their own behavior. They are capable of kindness and consideration. They form commitments and build relationships. They are not deliberately cruel, and they take no pleasure in inflicting pain. This is not so for the emotional predator, who is incapable of making a true commitment to another person—to a *relationship*—because their only commitment is to themselves, to their own needs. Relationships require compromise and, to an extent, sacrifice. If you want to build a relationship you must recognize that you cannot always have your own way, and must be capable of sacrificing your own desires at times in the interest of the relationship. Predators never willingly sacrifice or put others' needs ahead of their own.

You are best off learning to identify the above warning signs and taking them seriously if you want to avoid the worst possible mistake, which is to get entangled with an emotional predator.

***

Before committing to a relationship, you should also consider how insecure your potential partner is. Insecurity can make or break a relationship, and it can usually be identified if you know what you are looking for.

Insecurity rarely rears its ugly head at the outset of a relationship, when both people, after all, are putting their best foot forward. Only the most insecure people will become overly possessive, jealous, or distrustful from the beginning. If this does happen, though, you'd be wise to give that some serious thought. As one woman put it after deciding that one date with a new suitor was enough for her: "First he told me, about halfway through dinner, that jealousy was an issue for him. By the time they served dessert he was asking me how many sexual partners I'd had. Right then something inside me said that this would be our first and last date."

If someone you are interested in acts in a distrustful, controlling way from the very beginning of a relationship, or if they demand constant attention, that should be a tip-off to you that you are probably dealing with some pretty intense insecurity. Insecurity that is that obvious should be a sign to get out!

As you know by now, insecurity shows up in a person's attitude toward themselves and in certain behaviors. Just as you can't (or at least shouldn't) judge a book by its cover, you can't tell if the person you've just started dating is insecure by what kind of job they have or how they look. You need to look deeper than that.

Insecurity affects the way we see the world. The insecure person views the world in a distorted way. The more insecure you are, the stronger your distortions will be. What are these distortions? By now you also know that they have a lot to do with the expectations you (or your potential partner) have for a relationship. These expectations exert a strong influence on how you relate to each other. Unrealistic expectations set the insecure person up for continual disappointment and lead a relationship down the path to chronic stress and conflict. Often, insecure people look for reasons to distrust and to feel let down. They become unreasonably jealous and possessive. They are also self-conscious and extremely self-critical. Their self-doubts drive them to seek constant approval and attention. If they don't get it, they may blame the other person's "inadequacy" instead of their own unrealistic expectations.

Insecure people also seek out partners who they think will make up for something that has been missing in their lives. The problem is that insecurity operates on a deep level. The exact causes for a person's insecurity are often more or less unconscious, in that they haven't thought about the experiences that made them insecure for a long time and have never made a connection between these experiences and the expectations they bring into their adult relationships. Very often the need to compensate for their wounds takes precedence over all other considerations, so that an insecure person may jump into a relationship without taking the time to look at it in perspective. Despite their basic distrust they can be easily taken advantage of by someone who reads their insecurity and comes on to them with what they've been unconsciously craving: constant attention and approval. Of course, what seems too good to be true usually is; but insecure people often don't seem to realize this.

* * *

If insecurity describes someone you're seriously considering committing to, you need to understand that their insecurity will be a problem. Unless they recognize and choose to actively work on it, their insecurity could very well destroy the relationship in the long run. Don't assume that your love alone will heal insecurity. It is equally (or more) likely, in fact, that this person's insecurity will wear out your love for them long before your love heals their insecurity. Don't try to convince yourself that their expectations will go away if you only love this person enough. There is no way you will be able to live up to unconscious, unrealistic expectations. Similarly, don't assume that someone will outgrow their insecurity. Insecurity can be conquered, but it won't just disappear.

* * *

If you suspect that someone you are seriously interested in is suffering from some severe insecurity, the first thing you can do is talk to them about it. Chances are one reason you're drawn to them is that you sense some qualities within them—sensitivity, most likely—that you like a great deal. But the chances are that those desirable qualities are also buried beneath a layer of insecurity. At times when this person is feeling most insecure, the qualities in them that you've been most attracted to may all but disappear. What you may see at those times is only their jealousy, distrust, and neediness.

Confronting someone about insecurity is not necessarily easy. First of all, they may not understand what you're talking about. Second, they may take it as a criticism and react defensively. It's best to start off, therefore, on a positive note. Share with this person the qualities you see in them that you find attractive. Tell them how much you value their sensitivity, gentleness, consideration, or whatever it is that has drawn you to them.

That part should be easy. I don't know anyone who doesn't like a compliment, even if they pretend otherwise. The next step is more difficult. That step is to share with them some of the things they say or do that make you uncomfortable—that push you away instead of drawing you into the relationship. Keep this list *short*. Don't write down a list of twenty interactions that have bothered you and then present them, like a prosecutor presenting an indictment to a defendant. Better to choose two or three examples of the kinds of interactions that make you feel stifled or irritated.

Next, wait for a response. Don't rush to convince the other person that you're right about them. Give them some time to think about it; in fact, you might even suggest that they take some time to think about what you've said before responding. Remember: insecure people hate conflict. Any perception on their part that you may be attacking them will probably trigger a fight or a flight response. It's better to give the insecure person the message that you do not expect an immediate reaction or want them to defend or justify themselves. Then, after some time has passed, just ask them to tell you what they thought about what you said. If they balk, it's time to say that you would like to hear what they have to say, and to try to set up a time to do that. Keep in mind that your primary goal is to open communication. Healing insecurity takes a while. It requires insight and acceptance on the part of the insecure person. The whole process depends, however, on communication.

FINDING THE RIGHT PERSON

Aside from avoiding predatory people, there are some ground rules that could be helpful to you as you evaluate potential partners. One of these is exactly *how* different the two of you are in terms of interpersonal sensitivity; the other is *why* you are attracted to someone if they are very different from you.

Before you look for Mr. or Ms. Right, it can be useful to take a moment to reflect on what a relationship means to you. We live at a time when the popular belief is that each of us as individuals needs to be pretty much self-sufficient. We teach our adolescents, boys and girls alike, that they will need to be competitive and employable in order to survive in the adult world, regardless of whether they are single or in a relationship. The very concept of *depending* on someone else, of *needing* someone else in order to achieve our potential or to become complete, has become almost a sign of an unhealthy personality. In many relationships people think of themselves as partners, but not in the sense of needing another person to feel whole or complete. On the contrary, we're told that we need to feel whole—complete—all by ourselves *before* we can make it in a relationship. The idea that relationships can complete us or that they can bring out the best in us seems to have been left behind in our rush toward self-sufficiency.

* * *

It wasn't all that long ago that people believed that a relationship—and marriage in particular—was something that could and should bring out qualities and potentials in us that we might never realize if we remained single. Early marriage manuals and commentators on relationships encouraged men and women to think of marriage as an institution that could bring out the best in them, and saw a marriage as something bigger—richer, deeper—than the individual personalities that made it up. These ideas, old-fashioned as they may be, may have relevance when you're out there looking for the right person for you.

Here is an example of one person's testimony to the advantages of marriage. It is a passage written by Alexis de Tocqueville in the 1800s:

> I cannot describe to you the happiness yielded in the long run by the habitual society of a woman, in whose soul all that is good in your own is reflected naturally, and even improved. When I say or do a thing which seems to me to be perfectly right, I read immediately in Marie's countenance an expression of proud satisfaction which elevates me; and so when my conscience reproaches me her face instantly clouds over. Although I have great power over her mind, I see with pleasure that she awes me; and so long as I love her as I do now I am sure that I shall never allow myself to be drawn into anything that is wrong.

De Tocqueville was expressing a belief that was common in his day: that none of us is, or can be, complete all by ourselves; rather, we must look to a relationship to help complete us. As far as he was concerned, this made perfect sense. His notions about what a good marriage could do for him extended even to his potential for leading a virtuous life. Today de Tocqueville might be labeled codependent, and his relationship with Marie might be called dysfunctional. He'd be much better off, some might say, not relying on anyone else to help him fulfill his potential or lead a life of virtue. He should be able to do this for himself.

***

Over the second half of the twentieth century our culture has undergone a sea change in virtually every way imaginable, beginning with the sex roles we expect men and women to fulfill. Not so very long ago we still held somewhat different expectations for men and women. They are reflected in the lyrics of a popular song from the 1960s, titled "Five O'Clock World," by Allen Reynolds:

It's a five o'clock world when the whistle blows
 No one owns a piece of my time.
And there's a long haired girl who waits I know
 To ease my troubled mind.
In the shelter of her arms everything's okay
She talks and the world goes slippin' away.

Today we expect men and women alike to be able to survive in the world of work, which in the new millennium is an environment marked by intense competition driven by a global economy. On average, people work longer hours today than their parents or grandparents did. For men and women alike today, there is no one waiting at home for them at five o'clock to ease their worried minds or to make everything okay. These days, it seems, it's a five o'clock world for all of us, man and woman alike.

* * *

Regardless of all the changes we've seen in what men and women do—and regardless of how old the concept of a relationship bringing out the best in us and completing us is—in my mind it still deserves consideration. We may choose to define mental health today as being self-sufficient, but is this necessarily so? Could it be that we need to see it that way because of the way we are expected to live?

* * *

If you are looking for the right relationship for you, consider what I said earlier: that a good relationship should have a *personality* and a life of its own. Its personality is greater than the sum of its individual parts. Its life needs to be nourished through commitment, compromise, and sometimes through sacrifice on the part of both partners, if it is to thrive. Such a relationship, however, has the power to extend us, complete us, and bring out the best in us.

* * *

How does all of this apply to interpersonal sensitivity? Well, for one thing, it suggests that a relationship between two tenderhearted people, or between two tough-hearted people, is not necessarily the ideal. Such relationships may do fine; on the other hand, there may be something to gain when people who are somewhat different commit to a relationship. If they work together successfully, and if their differences are not too great, their differences can become a strength for the *relationship*. It is in this sense that a relationship can *extend* both people who are partners to it. It is in this way that a relationship can be greater than the sum of its parts. For this to happen, though, two things are necessary. First, the differences between partners cannot be *overwhelmingly* great. De Tocqueville and his beloved Marie, for example, were no doubt different people, with their unique personalities; yet I believe they must have had temperaments that were not too far apart. In my experience this is true for others as well: to be successful as a couple, partners cannot be so different in their natural temperaments as to be like night and day. Huge differences may be cause for curiosity and attraction, but they are also a poor predictor that a relationship will be fulfilling in the long run. Over time, the differences between a very tenderhearted person and a very tough-hearted one—the profoundly different ways in which they perceive and respond to the world—cannot help but introduce some tension, and potentially build alienation, in a relationship. Some greater common ground, temperamentally speaking, is a better bet for a long-term relationship. So, although differences can potentially add to, and not detract from, a relationship, it may be important to assess just *how* different you and a potential partner are when looking for your emotional mate.

The second requirement is that both partners be secure enough to be able to commit, and since partners are bound to have some differences in temperament, to be able to appreciate these differences and how they can work for them as a couple. This brings us back to the issue of insecurity. No one, of course, is perfectly secure. That is to say, most of us are at least a little insecure. What is needed for success in a relationship is not that a person become totally secure before they embark on it, but only that they have some insight and be actively working on reducing the negative impact that insecurity has on relationships.

***

When Jerry started out in counseling he was insecure. Judging from his outward appearances, though, few people would have guessed that he was insecure, or even sensitive. Through his twenties he had earned a living as a lumberjack, and he looked every bit the part, with a tall, sturdy build, a thick neck, and a short red beard. Jerry's passion was the outdoors. Hiking and canoeing were his favorite activities. His knowledge of birds and local wildlife was impressive; and his dream was to own a home surrounded by a forest.

Beneath this rugged exterior, though, there was a sensitive soul. For example, Jerry was introspective. He enjoyed reading about the outdoors as much as he enjoyed being there. He liked poetry and had even tried his hand at writing some. Despite his love for the woods and his comfort being by himself, like other interpersonally sensitive men and women he was a person who had many attachments to people, places, and things. His closest friends had been his friends for many years. He stayed in touch with them, saw them regularly, and was Uncle Jerry to their children, who looked forward to his unique and thoughtful Christmas presents. He was a kind, considerate person. Yet Jerry was also insecure, and his insecurity had caused him trouble in relationships.

Thanks to his determination and hard work, over a period of a couple of years Jerry made headway in healing his insecurity. The effects of his improved self-esteem and increased self-confidence had been most evident in his job. For a long time Jerry had been an underachiever, not for any lack of talent but because of his insecurity. He was overly cautious, sensitive to criticism, and defensive. I was sure this came across to others as a lack of confidence—a sure career stopper. He was highly self-critical, and overly critical of others as well, both of which undermined his effectiveness as a leader.

One result of his insecurity was that Jerry had reached a ceiling, in terms of both responsibility and salary, in his career. That was actually the reason he originally sought counseling. His issues around relationships came up only later. He had successfully worked on his insecurity to the point where he had been a team leader on two successful projects. After that he was promoted to a level where he was now benefiting from the profit sharing and stock options that were available to managers in his company.

For Jerry the healing process began as he was able to reevaluate and modify his expectations for himself. He would ruminate over the slightest mistake. Often these supposed mistakes were not even noticed by others. He expected himself, I said, to be perfect, and he would torture himself when he wasn't. Naturally, this was often. As we challenged these expectations, which Jerry was not consciously aware of, he was gradually able to become first more forgiving, then more supportive, of himself. As he was able to recognize his own efforts and praise his own successes more, he became less dependent on the approval of others for his self-esteem.

In time Jerry's acute self-consciousness eased up. Also, as he became more positive about himself, he was able to be more positive about others. He became less tentative, more self-assured. When he got his first team leader assignment he found it relatively easy and natural to use praise and encouragement to build team spirit and motivation. All in all, things had improved considerably for him in this sphere of his life.

* * *

Over the time we worked together I also witnessed Jerry begin and end several relationships. All but one of these had struck me as poor matches for Jerry, mostly because of a lack of common interests and goals, but also because a couple of the women had struck me as too tough-hearted for Jerry's sensitive nature. A pattern emerged in these relationships, one in which I felt that Jerry tried to accommodate the woman's needs, usually at the expense of his own. So long as *she* wanted the relationship, he felt obliged to work on it. He avoided conflict; but he also began to build up stores of resentment. At the same time, he invariably found himself troubled by jealousy, and more and more would seek the woman's approval. These, of course, were signs of his insecurity at work.

Usually, Jerry hung around in a relationship even after he knew, on a gut level, that it wasn't the right one for him, not necessarily because there was anything wrong with the woman but because the relationship wasn't a good fit. But Jerry would try to talk himself into the fit, because that was easier than being assertive and breaking it off. Although he tried to convince me otherwise, I saw him hanging on simply to avoid a possible confrontation or because he wouldn't want to hurt the woman's feelings. Instead, he'd question his own feelings, second-guessing what his own gut told him. This is not a good way to choose a mate, but Lord only knows how many insecure men and women have done just that—ignore what their hearts and guts tell them, and try to talk themselves into something rather than risk a confrontation.

How did Jerry end these relationships? In general, very indirectly, and over an excruciatingly long period of time. He'd begin the process of breaking away by gradually withdrawing. He'd make up excuses for why he couldn't see the woman as often as before. He'd extend business trips in order to stay away from home as long as possible. He'd pretend to be sick, or tired, or beg off on the grounds of some big project that he had to work on at home. Sometimes this was enough: not a few women eventually read between the lines and did the same, gradually tapering off the relationship. Others, though, could be more confrontational; and at these times Jerry would truly squirm. Only if pressed would he abandon his indirect approach to ending a relationship and admit that he felt it wasn't the right one for him. Even then, he never came out and said it as directly as that. More typically, he'd blame himself, saying that it was his problem. For example, he'd say that he wasn't ready for a commitment, when the truth was he didn't feel comfortable with the relationship as a match.

One of my goals for Jerry was to help him detach emotionally to some degree from the person he was in a relationship with, at least enough to focus a little less on her feelings and a little more on his own. He needed to stop asking himself so much whether he *should* feel this way or that, and allow that his feelings were valid. If he didn't want to do something, for example, he should stop questioning whether it was okay to feel that way, and just feel it. A second goal was to encourage him to give a voice to his feelings, instead of holding back, even if that meant expressing something that the woman he was dating might not want to hear.

***

In contrast to the others, one of relationships that Jerry mentioned sounded promising. For one thing, this was a woman who shared some of his interests. She also struck me, from the way Jerry described her, as a fairly sensitive person, like him. But here again, Jerry's insecurity did him in. How? Because this time he waited too long, was too hesitant to pursue, and was hobbled by his fears that something would go wrong, or that he'd wake up one morning to discover that she didn't love him anymore. So Jerry hung back instead of moving forward, and the woman eventually gave up and moved on. Through watching Jerry lose this potentially good relationship, I witnessed firsthand this side of insecure people: how trusting their own feelings and acting on them assertively is such a difficult thing for them to do.

Again, as is true for all insecure people, Jerry secretly harbored some pretty unrealistic expectations for relationships. When I suggested this and pointed out how these expectations were played out in his attitudes and behavior, he was genuinely surprised. I wasn't, though, since these expectations rarely exist on a conscious level in the insecure person's mind. Since they aren't looking at their behavior and attitudes in terms of expectations, they don't interpret them in this way. However, once they do make this connection, they usually can see the connection between expectations and behavior. At that point the doorway to change opens.

Jerry's insecurity, complete with its self-doubt and unrealistic expectations, popped up again a few months later, when he was introduced to Liz, the recently divorced sister of one of his best friends. The two of them had hit it off from the beginning. Jerry described Liz as someone with whom he felt extremely comfortable from their first meeting. "I found that I could just be completely myself with her," he said. "I found myself not feeling self-conscious at all, which is unusual for me as you know, especially when I begin dating a new woman. It turns out she has a great sense of humor and is very down-to-earth. She's got a good job, and friends, and she likes a lot of the same things that I do."

Then Jerry's insecurity kicked in. I noticed that he started coming to me, week after week, with various issues he wanted to discuss about his relationship with Liz. From everything he said, I had the strong impression that this relationship was a very good one for both of them. First and foremost, they were having a good time together. They laughed a lot, shared common interests (including hiking *and* canoeing!), and enjoyed talking to each other. Liz had a six-year-old son from her previous marriage, and she'd let Jerry know that she was interested in having one, and possibly two, more children. Jerry had talked with me about his desire to have a family, and had even gone through a painful breakup with a woman who, though compatible with him in some other ways, was firm in her desire not to have any children.

From where I sat it was hard for me to see any areas in which Jerry and Liz were significantly incompatible. Sure, they weren't clones. She was more outgoing than he was, for example, and she was a good money manager. She also had interests and commitments that he didn't share. For example, she was close to her brother and sister and her nieces and nephews. She had already made it clear that if she and Jerry ever did get together she would want to see her family on a regular basis. This had been an issue in her marriage, she said, because her husband had not liked her family from the beginning. He put them down and gave her a hard time whenever she wanted to see them. By the end of the marriage it had become a sore point between them.

As Jerry told me about this, he looked tense. "So, what's the issue?" I asked. I knew very well that Jerry, too, had many close friends. They functioned as an extended family that he saw regularly. He said he was worried, though, about how Liz would feel if he didn't want to go along every time she wanted to visit her family, who lived several hours away by car. He wondered if it could become a source of tension between them. "I like her family very much," he said, "but I still do a fair amount of traveling for work, you know? And I know that if

I'm away from home for a few days, it's very likely that I won't want to drive several hours that weekend. I'll get home and just want to stay there."

I told Jerry I could understand his sentiments, and suggested that he check out this concern with Liz. Would she expect him to accompany her every time she visited her sisters?

When we met two weeks later, Jerry told me he had spoken with Liz about his concern, and specifically about her expectations for his involvement with them. She'd told him she would understand if he didn't want to go with her every time she saw her family. She explained that she had only intended to let Jerry know that she would want to continue the kind of regular contact she had now with her family. They were important to her, and she didn't ever want that to be an issue that could come between her and a partner again, as it had before. I asked Jerry how he felt about that response. Fine, he said. Indeed, he did seem more relaxed, at least for the moment.

The next issue Jerry brought up concerned Liz's son. He was worried, he told me, that the boy wouldn't like him. I pointed out that the boy seemed to like Jerry well enough now. "But what happens if we get together, and then he doesn't like me?" Jerry asked.

"So, what would happen then?" I asked. "What's your concern?"

Jerry replied that he was worried that any tension between him and Liz's son would put her in the middle, and potentially strain their relationship.

"And how do you think she would handle that?" I asked. "Do you think she would choose her son over you?"

From the way Jerry reacted I could see that I'd guessed correctly. He feared that Liz would abandon him if she were ever in a position of having to choose between Jerry and her son. Again, I suggested that perhaps Jerry should bring it up directly with Liz. I pointed out that Liz could avoid being placed in that situation, unless something extreme, like physical abuse, was involved. She could do this by telling Jerry and her son that she loved them both but had different relationships with them; therefore they were commitments that could not be compared or pitted against each other. If either of them tried to do that, she could simply say that she wanted both relationships and would not allow herself to be forced to choose between them.

Jerry came back two weeks later and reported that Liz had said pretty much the same thing that I had said, albeit using somewhat different words. Then he started to bring up two more issues. "I've noticed that Liz is a lot better about managing her money than I am," he said. "And it's pretty obvious that she's a lot more organized than I am."

I interrupted. "So, are you worried now that *these* differences between you could become a problem?" I asked, looking Jerry in the eye. "Do you remember," I continued, "the discussions we've had about your hidden expectations for relationships?" He looked back at me and nodded in a way that told me he knew exactly what I was talking about.

"You know, Jerry," I said, "I think you need to look at the role that your own insecurity may be playing in these 'issues' that you keep bringing up. It's natural to feel nervous when you're standing on the brink of a major commitment. But it seems to me that the theme here is your fear that you could lose Liz's love and affection. So you're hedging by bringing up—even making up—these issues. On some level it's as though you're looking for a guarantee here—an insurance policy to cover your insecurity. Maybe we all secretly wish for the perfect woman: one who will never let us down or get angry at us, who will love us and us alone. In your case, maybe you're unconsciously looking for someone who will never abandon you, as both of your parents did on account of their alcoholism. It's understandable from the point of view of the abandonment you felt as a child. But it's also unrealistic. It's part of your insecurity. Neither of us can tell for sure what would happen if you and Liz got together, or had children. Hopefully, you'd be happy. It certainly sounds like you're happy now, and compatible. But I think I can guarantee that each of you will find that your relationship competes with at least some other commitments now and then, and that sooner or later each of you will do *something* that will hurt the other. If you allow yourself unconsciously to expect perfection, then you're sure to be disappointed, and very likely you'll start building up resentments."

***

I was convinced that Jerry's list of worries would never have ended if I hadn't spoken up about how they seemed related more to his own insecurities than to any significant differences between him and Liz. My gut feeling was that no matter how compatible Jerry and Liz were, no matter how much she loved him, what he secretly wished for was that written guarantee that he would never be hurt. He couldn't have that guarantee, I said. None of us can. The only sane choice, then, assuming he wanted a relationship, was to let go of his unconscious, unrealistic expectations.

Jerry and Liz did end up together. There was one experience in particular that made a big difference for Jerry, and he related it to me the next time we met. This experience, simple as it was, proved to be a real breakthrough for him. It enabled him to overcome his hesitation, rise above his insecurity, and make a decision. It happened when he, Liz, and her son decided to go camping together over a long weekend. They took Jerry's canoe, along with his camping and fishing equipment. It was the first time the three of them had been alone together for that length of time. They spent four days camping, canoeing, hiking, cooking, talking, and playing games on the banks of a beautiful lake.

Jerry spoke about how he and Liz worked well together as a team, and how her son had also fit in so well. "It was really great being together like that, the three of us. We just meshed well together."

"Like a family?" I offered.

Jerry smiled. "Yeah. We worked together, had fun together. I got to know Liz's son a whole lot better, and vice versa. We really hit it off. He seemed genuinely interested in learning as much as I could teach him about the outdoors." The whole experience, Jerry said, was engrossing. And that was what gave it its impact. "It didn't hit me until two or three days afterward," he said, "that I didn't think about *myself* once during that entire weekend. Not my anxieties, not my doubts. I wasn't burdened with self-consciousness at all. I was completely absorbed in what was going on. I'll tell you, that was refreshing. It was liberating. You know that I've always been self-conscious.

Sometimes I think that at least half of my problem in life is that I'm too self-conscious. Its almost like I'm self-centered or something."

I offered Jerry an alternative view of his self-consciousness: that it wasn't self-centeredness but insecurity. He wasn't vain; rather, he was always watching himself, being eternally vigilant for any flaw or mistake. But something about those four days, I suggested, had allowed him to slip out of his insecurity, and along with it went his self-consciousness.

I have heard breakthrough stories like Jerry's from many insecure people, and the theme is always the same. Feeling respected and valued, on a deep level, by someone they care about helps to dissolve, at least temporarily, the self-consciousness that plagues insecure people. If they can reflect on this kind of experience, as Jerry did, it can open the way to a new way of looking at themselves and others.

In Jerry's case, their camping experience, among other things, convinced him that Liz was a special woman, that her son was a special boy, and that the opportunity to link his life with theirs was one he'd be a fool to pass up. "I've decided I'm not going to sit on this one and ponder it until I've lost it," he said. "Liz and I have got a good thing here, for both of us, and I think we both know it." As he spoke, Jerry's voice was firm, without a hint of doubt or hesitation. I had a good feeling about him then, and also about his relationship with Liz. It struck me that this relationship was indeed bringing out the best in Jerry, and fulfilling him in ways that his single life never could. By incorporating their differences as well as their shared interests into their relationship, and building on them, I felt, this couple could have a really good life together.

* * *

Finding your emotional mate is partly a matter of learning to avoid the wrong one and partly a matter of recognizing it when a good candidate comes along. When thinking about committing, there are a number of factors to consider. First, just how interpersonally sensitive are you, as compared to your potential partner? Is the difference between you a major one, or is it a gap that can be bridged? Is it even possible that the differences in your *individual* temperaments could make you stronger as a *couple*?

Major insecurity in one or both partners can be more of a threat to a relationship than any real differences in temperament. The material in this book can help an individual decide if insecurity may be a factor in their relationships. It also provides guidelines for working on insecurity. The man or woman who is able to recognize his or her own insecurity and understand how it operates, and who can make a commitment to overcoming it, is in a much better place to make a relationship work than is someone who is either blind to their own insecurity or unwilling to work on it.

12

Raising Sensitive (Not Insecure) Children

John's life was a painful testimony to the destructive power of insecurity. He was the youngest of three children, and the only boy. His mother had abandoned the family when John was barely two. According to John, his father's alcoholism had most likely contributed to his mother's decision to bolt. Regardless of her reasons, though, her decision still left John and his sisters without even one effective parent. A month later his paternal grandmother moved in. She was responsible, but she was also old and ill. For the next year she provided stability, regular meals, and clean clothes to wear, but not much in the way of individual attention or affection. "I remember she'd be in bed by seven, eight o'clock at the very latest, every night," he said. "Of course, she also must have gotten up every morning by five in order to have our breakfasts ready, our lunches made, our clothes all laid out. In that way she was good to us. But there wasn't any kind of a *relationship* there, between any of us and her, if you know what I mean."

After a year or so John's father remarried. His stepmother, like his mother, was a nondrinker; but according to John she was also a very cool, detached person. And selfish. "She took care of herself first," John said. "I guess that was the price my old man had to pay for loving his booze. Outside of his booze, he never did get very much of what he wanted."

Like most children, including both of his sisters, young John initially reacted to being abandoned with panic and extreme distress. He remembered how impatient his father was with this, especially in him, and how he once snapped, "Stop whining and get over it!" Which John did—or at least the whining stopped. He never got close to his stepmother, but then neither did anyone else in the family. As far as anyone could tell, John got over his grief and just went on with his life—until he was about twelve years old.

Earlier in this book I made the point that adults often mistakenly believe that the grief that children experience when they lose an important attachment gets resolved easily: that they simply get over the loss and get used to living without that attachment, as though it was never there to begin with. Nothing could be further from the truth. Many children, and perhaps boys more so than girls, can suffer lasting emotional damage. Certainly some research on the effects of children's separation from their mothers has suggested that boys may take this even harder than girls. But the fact is it's hard on children regardless of their sex. Also, the fact that children tend to suppress their pain, anxiety, and anger may give others the impression that all is well when in fact the problem has simply gone underground, as it did for John.

By the time he reached puberty the pain and anger that John had long ago buried deep inside him began to erupt. However, it would be years before he or anyone would draw a connection between what had happened to him as a child and the behavior that caused him so much trouble later on. It started with rebelliousness. It wasn't that John was particularly tough or aggressive; but he began skipping school and letting his homework go. In a single year his grades plummeted from A's and B's to D's and F's. His stepmother occasionally got on his back about it, supported halfheartedly by his father; but mostly no one cared. Besides, they had no real relationship with John and didn't know what to do to influence him, other than scold him and issue dire warnings about what happened to people who didn't finish high school. John knew very well what happened to them. His own father had never finished high school; nor had his uncle. Both were alcoholics, and both had done no better than unskilled factory work all their lives.

In high school John started drinking and using drugs. At the same time, his rebelliousness took a cynical turn. He became the editor of an underground student newspaper that published anarchic essays and criticized virtually anything and everything about the school administration. He made friends, but like him they were alienated—from the mainstream student body as much as from the faculty and administration. They dressed in a common way that identified them as a clique and set them apart from other students. They had unique preferences in music, in what they liked to read, and the way they wore their hair.

Then, on the first day of his senior year, John met Judy and fell immediately in love. She was a year younger and a year behind him in school. She was not in his clique and didn't want to be. Their chance meeting in a study hall, however, would change his life forever.

Judy challenged John. On the one hand she told him, repeatedly, that she thought he was very intelligent and creative; on the other hand, she asked him why he wanted to be such a freak. Partly because of his attraction, but also because he sensed that Judy really cared for him, John tolerated this; more than that, he absorbed it.

In many ways John's senior year was the happiest time of his life. It was also a time when he began to move out from beneath the shadow of insecurity. His grades that year were the best they'd been since he was in fifth grade and more accurately reflected his actual ability. He got a part-time job, cut way down on his drinking and drug use, and saved enough to be able to buy an old but serviceable car. Judy and he spent endless hours sitting in it by the edge of a local river, talking, listening to music, and eventually, making love. John described himself as completely happy.

Then, less than a month after John graduated, Judy abruptly broke off the relationship. Without warning, but with obvious difficulty, she told John that she'd decided she didn't want to be tied down during her senior year. She told him she still loved him, but she felt that she was just too young to make a commitment.

John, who all this time had been thinking about the future and fantasizing about marriage, was devastated. He started drinking very heavily. In his own words, "I drank whatever I could get my hands on, as much as I could get my hands on, and whenever I could." He said he was oblivious much of the time. A month later he was arrested on charges of sexually assaulting a woman he met at a bar. He didn't know her at all, he said, and the only thing he could recall was following her when she left the bar, sometime after midnight.

The sexual assault got John a prison sentence. He served five years, and when he got out his first stop was at an AA meeting. By the time he came to see me he'd had nine years of sobriety: the five he'd served in prison, plus four more since. His reason for seeking therapy, he said, was depression. His AA friends were aware of it, he said, and his sponsor had strongly encouraged him to get into therapy, predicting that if he didn't, John was setting himself up for a slip.

Indeed, John told me that he found himself thinking about drinking more often. He described episodes of driving around for hours, struggling with an urge to stop at a liquor store. So far he'd passed them by. In addition, he had significant symptoms of depression, including a general loss of energy and motivation, trouble sleeping, a weight loss of twenty pounds over the last six months, and most ominously, feeling at times that life wasn't worth living. I also discovered that since leaving prison, he'd had three relationships, all of them brief, and none of them satisfying. He volunteered that he agreed with something his closest AA friends were saying: that he seemed to deliberately choose women who he didn't feel particularly drawn to; that way he couldn't get so hurt when things didn't work out. Of course, there was no way they could work out, since John wasn't particularly attracted to these women in the first place!

Although John was well along the road to recovery from alcoholism, he hadn't yet taken the first step on the road to recovery from his insecurity. Any progress he'd made in that last year of high school had long since withered and disappeared. As we spoke it was also clear that he was completely unaware of any connections between his childhood, his relationship with Judy, and the sexual assault. He'd turned to alcohol to kill the pain; but it was that same alcohol that had set free the demons inside him—that enabled him to vent his anger through a sexual assault on a woman he didn't know but who paid the price for all the anger and pain he'd kept bottled up for years. He was sensitive and bright, but much of what drove him lay deep in his unconscious.

***

The obvious question, reading John's story, is this: could this have been prevented? Was there any way that the chain of events that seemed to lead so inexorably from John's childhood experiences of abandonment (by both his parents) to the rape that landed him in jail and made him a marked man for the rest of his life could have been broken? More generally, are there things that we can do—as parents and therapists, or even as teachers and clergy—to either prevent insecurity or at least lessen its potential for destructiveness? I believe the answer to all of these questions is yes.

BUILDING AND PROTECTING AN ATTACHMENT NETWORK

To prevent the kind of tragedy that happened to John, the first thing we need to appreciate is how important it is for a child, regardless of how tenderhearted or tough-hearted they may be by nature, to have a stable network of people, places, and things that they can become attached to, and *stay* attached to, until they are ready to begin breaking away. What do I mean by a network? I mean a whole set of people, of routines, and of places that remain relatively stable and constant throughout early childhood.

Children love nothing better than stability. It is perhaps the best insurance against insecurity. Sure, children are curious. Sure, some of them tend to wander from their mothers sooner, and farther, than others do. And differences in interpersonal sensitivity do become apparent early on. Still, despite these individual differences, we make a big mistake if we think of young children as infinitely adaptable to change, because they most certainly are not. Similarly, we make a big mistake if we think that children recover easily from broken connections or attachments, abuse or neglect, because they don't. As the examples in this book attest, too often children's grief and anxiety merely goes underground, to reemerge later, sometimes much later, with devastating results.

I was once approached by a young working mother who asked for my help in dealing with the administration of the school district where she lived. Vicky's son, Jesse, had just turned four and was scheduled to begin a prekindergarten program. Because both she and her husband had to work full-time, Jesse had been placed in a day care center starting at age one and a half. Vicky had taken great care in selecting this center. She made sure that it was licensed, she interviewed the staff, and she spent several hours talking with the director. Most important, from her perspective, she checked to see how long the staff had worked there. She chose a center with a very stable staff, and she made sure that Jesse stayed in it.

Although he'd had some adjustment problems at first, over time Jesse had become very much attached to his day care center. He was attached to the teacher who'd been his primary caretaker for nearly two and a half years. He was attached, too, to several of the other children who'd been his peer group all that time. Beyond that, he was attached to the place itself. This became clear when a new staff member—an intern—had decided to do some rearranging of things. She not only moved things about but decided on her own initiative to put away several old toys that seemed to be broken beyond repair.

When Jesse and the other children arrived at the center the next day, the first thing they did was pause and look around, taking in the changes. Then a few of them, Jesse included, began to systematically move as many things as they could find *back* to their original places. When Jesse could not find his favorite toy, he asked for it. The intern tried to interest him in something new, to no avail. He just wasn't interested. Worse, he became irritable. Soon, several others started getting irritable, too. When the director arrived, about half an hour later, she quickly assessed the situation and took the intern aside. A few minutes later they emerged from a storage room carrying the old toys. Jesse and his friends literally jumped for joy.

Vicky did her best to see to it that her own work schedule was as regular as possible. She did everything she could, for example, to minimize the number of times someone other than she had to pick Jesse up from day care; and she told her employer that she would not generally be available for overtime. Under this set of conditions, Jesse thrived.

Then, all of a sudden, the conditions that had proved so beneficial to Jesse's development were threatened. The school district informed Vicky, via a form letter, that Jesse would not be permitted, as she'd requested, to attend the prekindergarten program that was located less than a mile from his day care center. Vicky had made that request because it would allow Jesse to stay in his day care center, where he could be dropped off every day by the school bus. Instead, the letter indicated that Jesse would have to attend another prekindergarten program. This other program was located closer to his home, but many miles from his day care center. Attending this other program would mean that Vicky would have to find another day care center for Jesse, since there was no way that the school could drop him off at his regular day care center if he attended the prekindergarten they had scheduled him for.

Vicky and her husband reacted to the letter from the school by writing a polite request that an exception be made, allowing Jesse to attend the program closer to his day care center. Their request was denied. They then requested a meeting with the school superintendent. A meeting was granted; the superintendent listened politely, then said he would get back to them. Two weeks later they got another rejection. In his letter the superintendent wrote that he did not see any reason to change school policy. Children were sent to the prekindergarten program that was closest to their home address, he wrote, not to the program that was closest to day care, to their parents' place of work, or anywhere else. That was their policy, period.

Vicky and her husband came to me to talk about Jesse. When I met Jesse I discovered a happy, friendly boy—a child who struck me as the product of a functional family. Vicky and her husband were happy and were in the process of trying to expand their family. Jesse, meanwhile, was verbal and energetic, and from what I could tell he was developing normally. After our meeting I wrote to the school superintendent, expressing my support for Vicky and her husband's request that Jesse be allowed to attend the prekindergarten program that was close to his day care, which would allow him to stay there. The response I got shocked me. I got a letter—a very cool letter—stating that in order to consider Jesse's parents' request, I would have to document the nature of any emotional problems Jesse had that would indicate that it would be harmful for him to attend the program that school policy required him to attend.

This response struck me as so off the mark that I didn't know whether to laugh or to get angry. I did a little of both, I think. Were they serious? Was the school really saying that Jesse would have to be dysfunctional *before* they'd consider his parents' request? Did they really think it was more important to follow some policy based on geography, rather than making decisions based on what was best for a child's development? Was it really worth turning Jesse's life upside down just to avoid making an exception?

I wrote back to the school administration. This time I made it clear that the purpose of my initial letter was not to suggest that there was anything wrong with Jesse; on the contrary, he was a very happy, bright, and well-adjusted boy. The point in my writing, rather, was to urge the school district not to do anything to disrupt Jesse's development. I was coming from a *preventive* perspective, I said, not a clinical one.

It turned out that my second letter, combined with constant pressure from Jesse's parents, won the day. Vicky got a letter from the superintendent that "under the circumstances" (it wasn't more specific than that), an exception to district policy would be granted, and Jesse would be allowed to attend prekindergarten at the site that would also enable him to stay with his day care program.

***

Although this story had a happy ending for Jesse, it points out how common it is for people—including, in this case, educators, who presumably understand child development—to assume that even young children are so adaptable that we can simply move them around, or change their environment, whenever it suits us, and that there will be no consequences. Just because a child, like Jesse, is developing normally, does that mean that they are infinitely adaptable? Should we test the limits of their resilience, or should we advocate for stability and security?

The attitude of the school system in this case may simply mirror our contemporary attitude toward adults and families. Global competition has gradually given rise to the mobile society and, increasingly, to the global family. Most adults expect their lives to be anything but stable. They expect to be moved around, either to advance their own economic situation or else to satisfy the company's needs. Connections to community, church, family, and friends are growing ever more tentative. Families cannot realistically expect to remain put; beyond that, we expect them to endure disruption and change without any consequences. We even go so far as to suggest that people who resist change are somehow dysfunctional. However, even supposedly positive changes—moving the family, for example, for a better job—may not be as benign as we'd like to think.

I believe we may have allowed ourselves to believe that children need a lot less stability than they do. The popular idea that "they'll get over it" may be a tempting way to avoid confronting the consequences of the broken connections that children increasingly must deal with. That attitude may allow us to avoid thinking about the psychological implications of breaking up children's attachment networks; but I believe that it is wrong. I believe that living in a mobile society, where we all have fewer and fewer connections, makes it all the more important for parents to do whatever they can to insure that their children's lives are as stable as possible, and to allow them to form and maintain connections to people, places, and things. This will facilitate the development of their sense of personal security: their sense of who they are in relation to the world around them, and their worth as individuals. This is the foundation for healthy personality development. Showering children with material pleasures may soothe parents' consciences, but it will not make the effects of broken attachments go away; nor will it substitute for the sense of identity and worth that comes from having a long-standing network of stable attachments.

Despite the fact that economics required Vicky to move her son into full-time day care sooner than she would have liked, I admired her commitment to maintaining a stable attachment network for her son. She was committed to this, and tenacious in protecting it. On a gut level she knew that her son's healthy development was tied in part to the stable life that she and her husband had worked so hard to provide. It is too bad that parents like these must fight the system in order to provide stability for their children. Many parents do not wish to go to such lengths or may not possess the depth of conviction that Vicky and her husband did.

CREATING A FOUNDATION FOR SECURITY: RITES, RITUALS, AND TRADITIONS

Closely related to the need to maintain stability in a child's day-to-day life is the need to create and preserve a network of rites, rituals, and traditions within the family. Rites, rituals, and traditions are the glue that keeps a social group—whether it be a family, a religious community, or a whole society—together and bonded to one another. They provide the predictability, the stability, and the sense of belonging that are an antidote to insecurity.

Children thrive on ritual just as they thrive on stability. Change and surprise can be exciting for children, but as every parent knows, they can also be unnerving, and children definitely have a limited tolerance for them. In contrast, children look forward to family traditions and rituals with eager anticipation. Of course, there are those abused children who may very well have had their outlook on rituals and traditions clouded by virtue of their abuse. Not a few people I've met have told me stories about how they dreaded holidays, or Sunday afternoon dinners, because of the abuse that was associated with these occasions. Yet even these people, along with breaking the chain of abuse, often create and preserve rituals and traditions for their own children.

I am not talking here about trying to hide abuse behind family traditions or rituals. I am talking about what is best for children's development; and what is best is that they not be abused and that they also live a life filled with rituals and traditions, a life in which their developmental journey from into adulthood is celebrated through meaningful rites of passage.

The speed at which our culture has abandoned rites, rituals, and traditions is alarming from the point of view of children's psychological development. It is part of that sea change in our culture that I have mentioned at several points in this book, and that has dominated the second half of the twentieth century. Think back for a moment on your own childhood. Try to recall any family rituals that you remember. Rituals are generally small acts that are repeated frequently, often daily. They include things like kissing your parents good night, reading bedtime stories, or watching a particular television show together. Answer these questions:

* What rituals do you remember most?

* Can you recall the feelings you had about these rituals? For example, did you look forward to them?

* How did you feel if one of your rituals had to be canceled for some reason?

Most people tell me that, as children, the idea of skipping a ritual would have made them uneasy at the least. Also, many people can clearly recall their reaction when, for one reason or another, a ritual had to be given up altogether. Death and divorce disrupt many rituals, but so do more subtle changes, such as a parent whose work hours change or who takes a job that requires a great deal of travel. Of course, some of these changes can't be avoided; but when they occur, it is wise to consider how children's rituals can be preserved. For example, who will tell the bedtime stories after Mom or Dad has to work nights? Or who will play a child's favorite game with them after their parents separate?

* * *

Let's turn our attention now to *traditions*. Think back on your own family's traditions when you were growing up. Traditions are similar to rituals, only bigger, more elaborate. They usually involve a group, especially the family, and sometimes the extended family. Traditions include holiday celebrations, vacations, and family activities. My own daughter looked forward in particular to Christmas Eve dinners and opening presents. Every year she made sure that my father—the designated Santa—sat in the same rocking chair and gave out the presents one at a time. Each year she would check ahead of time to be sure that Christmas Eve was "on," that everyone was coming who customarily came, especially her cousins. Invariably she'd also check with me to be sure that the menu included the same key items as it had all the years before.

Additional traditions we observed were a week in Maine every summer, in the same cabin. My daughter made sure that we did some of the same activities, year after year, like having tea and popovers on a lawn overlooking a lake in Acadia National Park, and climbing the same mountain to take in the same view together. It was obvious how important each of these traditions was to her.

Whereas rituals build connections between individuals, traditions build connections between members of the family as a whole. Rituals and traditions serve a common and vital psychological purpose: they create and maintain attachments and bonds between individuals. They give us a sense of place and importance. Like rituals, traditions work against chaos and broken connections—two major causes of insecurity. The main difference is that traditions operate on a larger scale than rituals. Both are important to a child's sense of security. Letting traditions slide, like being too busy to keep up rituals, usually instills a degree of discomfort in children, who will often protest loudly and clearly. It is the wise parent who hears these protests and does something about them.

If you are a parent, but for one reason or another have bad memories and feelings about your own family traditions (or if you never had them), you can be creative in creating traditions for your own family. In my own case, most of the core traditions that my daughter counted on were actually quite different from the ones I grew up with; only a few were similar. Interestingly, she would ask me about those traditions. "What did Grandma and Grandpa do on Christmas?" she would ask. "Did you open presents on Christmas Eve? Did you open them one at a time?" When I told her that, in fact, we didn't start doing that until I and my brothers were older, the news seemed to put her temporarily off balance. Then she decided that the way we did it was okay—as long as we didn't change it!

***

Still another way to facilitate bonding and guard against insecurity is to be found in *rites of passage*. Rites of passage are organized on an even grander scale than family traditions; often they are organized on the level of the community, or at the very least the extended family. Rites of passage are central to all organized religions, but there are also other kinds: graduations, sweet sixteen parties, marriages, and retirement parties, for example, are all rites of passage. Rites of passage represent the recognition by the extended family or the larger community that a person (or sometimes a couple) is making a transition from one stage of development to another. Often the transition is associated with added *rights,* balanced by added *responsibilities*.

Rites of passage mark the progress of our journey through life. At the same time they serve the function of bonding the individual to the extended family and the community, and of recognizing the individual's *importance* and *place* in both. Again, rites of passage, like family traditions, help the individual to develop a secure sense of who they are in relation to the world around them, and their value. In doing so they can help to inoculate children against insecurity.

Today, many of our older rites of passage have fallen by the wayside. Too often the parties we create bear no relation to any developmental transition; in other words, they may be a good time, but they fail to include anything that marks a change in status—the granting of new rights and the assignment of new responsibilities. It doesn't have to be that way. It is possible for any celebration, be it a sweet sixteen party or a high school graduation, to include the basic elements of a rite of passage. Those elements include a recognition that some change has occurred, or some goal attained. They also include recognition that the person has moved to a place in life that enjoys new rights, but also new responsibilities. Finally, the celebration can recognize the value of the individual to their family and their community. I knew one set of parents who ceremoniously "awarded" their daughter her driver's license, along with a key to an old but serviceable car they'd bought for her, as part of a sweet sixteen party. Along with that recognition of her new status, however, these same parents praised the fact that their daughter had maintained a B grade average through her freshman year in high school, which they'd told her she would need to do in order to have access to the car. This little example illustrates nicely the elements of a rite of passage, because it marks a developmental milestone and because it links added rights with added responsibilities. A surprising number of parents today hesitate to do this. Instead, they simply grant their children additional rights without balancing them with added responsibilities. Perhaps this is because our culture as a whole is losing sight of this concept of rites of passage and its function with respect to raising responsible citizens. Whatever the reason, the result is that some parents are raising children who have a sense of entitlement but no corresponding sense of responsibility.

***

Creating a lifestyle that is rich in rituals, traditions, and rites of passage is one powerful step that parents can take to help raise children who are secure. There is really no good substitute for them. They cannot be made up for, psychologically, by material things. Though we may be tempted to try to build our children's sense of worth through the things we give them, this will not make them more secure.

Through the observance of rituals, traditions, and rites of passage we provide children with a sense of their place in the world, and of their worth to others, that is based not on what they have but on who they are. To the extent that we must prepare our children to thrive in a world of hyperchange, in which their own nuclear families may be their sole sources of connectedness, teaching them the value of these things may be as important a gift to them as our love.

THE POWER OF ACCEPTANCE

I chose not to discuss differences in children's interpersonal sensitivity in this chapter until now. I did this deliberately. The above advice on creating and preserving an attachment network, and on maintaining rituals, traditions, and rites, is good psychological medicine not only for sensitive children but for *all* children. The consequences of failure to provide for children's needs in any of these areas may vary depending on how sensitive a child is, but they are never good.

If you happen to be the parent of a child who seems to be very interpersonally sensitive, then the first thing you can do is to underline all of the foregoing advice. You can expect your child to react even more than the average child will to disruptions in their connections to people, places, and things. You can expect them to react even more strongly to abuse or rejection; and you can expect them to show the effects of any absence or disruption of rites, rituals, and traditions in their lives.

One of the most subtle forms of rejection—one that many well-intentioned parents do not even recognize as being rejection—has to do with trying to change a child's basic temperament. The most common form of this that I've encountered is parents trying to make a sensitive child tougher. I worked with one father who, sensing his son's sensitivity, tried to do just this. He tried to make his son tougher by teaching him, for example, how to gut fish and by taking him deer hunting. Predictably, the boy soon lost interest in both fishing and hunting. Feeling rejected and frustrated, the father then berated the boy, calling him soft.

Trying to change someone's basic temperament—trying to make a tenderhearted person more tough-hearted—is kind of like trying to make a left-handed person into a right-handed person. People used to try to do that, too, with about as much success. For some reason, being left-handed was once thought to be undesirable. Left-handed children were placed into remedial programs whose goal was to make them right-handed. It's hard to imagine just how much damage was done to how many children's self-esteem by labeling their innate preference as a deficit and by forcing them to try to write, for hour after hour, with the hand that wasn't the one they naturally favored. Not surprisingly, the number of failures was huge.

Parents sometimes try to change a child's natural temperament in much the same way that people once tried to change handedness, and for much the same reasons. Some people tend to think of tender-heartedness as a flaw of some sort. They believe that being more tough-hearted is a better bet for getting along in the world. The father I just described, Dan, thought exactly this. He admitted to me that he was very concerned that his son's sensitivity would prove to be a handicap as he grew older. His own belief, based on the way he saw the world, was that only the tough survive. He truly cared about his son and very much wanted him not only to survive but to prosper. He earnestly believed that toughening up his son was the best way to do that. Sadly, the way he went about trying to help his son only made matters worse. The boy ended up feeling bad about himself, and their relationship deteriorated.

* * *

A tenderhearted child will perceive and react to being teased about their temperament as rejection. Worse still, it is perceived as a rejection of a core part of themselves that they instinctively know they can't really change. It is very different, for example, from being criticized for poor study habits, poor hygiene, or poor manners. All of these other areas are basically behaviors that can be changed, if a person wants to change them. In these areas it is a parent's responsibility to model, to monitor, and to correct. Not so for our children's God-given temperaments. If we come across as rejecting of these, we run the risk of damaging both their self-esteem and our relationships with them.

My advice to Dan was that he should trust in the fact that his son was attached to him and would naturally want to spend time with him. I encouraged him to accept his son's preferences, though, for which activities he wanted to share with his father. Finally, we talked frankly about the need to accept his son for who he was. Six months later Dan and his boy were doing things together regularly, whereas when he first met with me, Dan said that he and his son hadn't really shared any significant time together in well over a year. This change, I said, would not only help Dan's son but would inevitably make Dan a more effective parent, because his son was that much more attached to him.

***

The key to effective parenting lies in the parent-child bond. All of the advice in this chapter is aimed at building that bond. We know what children need most: nurturing, support, and also limits. Lack of discipline can be just as dangerous as lack of affection. All of these things, however, are made easier when there is a strong bond between parent and child. Bonding with a sensitive child is no different from bonding with any child. The basic ingredients are acceptance and involvement. Your sensitive child must learn to live with his or her sensitivity, to appreciate it, and if necessary to make sure that it is not exploited by others. He or she needs your acceptance and support in this, but not your efforts to change his or her disposition.

In preventing insecurity it is important to accept your child's disposition, even if you have concerns about it. Parents instinctively want to protect their children. Sometimes, if we sense that our child may be vulnerable, we may be tempted to respond in one of two ways. First, we may be tempted to shelter them. While this is an understandable urge, it is not a good idea to overprotect and shelter a child, even a very sensitive one. A better course of action is to build their sense of security. You can do that in part by following the advice in this chapter. There is no reason why a secure, sensitive child will be handicapped when it comes to having a fulfilling life. On the contrary, much of this book has been devoted to helping insecure people rediscover their sensitivity. It is insecurity that robs a person of their potential, not sensitivity. Sensitive people can be very successful, both in their careers and in their personal lives.

The other urge that a parent can have is what Dan did, which is to try to toughen up a child they perceive as sensitive. Ironically, this is likely to do just the opposite. By coming across as rejecting a child's basic nature, you run the risk of generating insecurity. Again, the better course is to accept, indeed appreciate, your child's sensitivity and to work to build the kind of family life that will promote both sensitivity and security.

Epilogue

By now you should have a better understanding of yourself, and perhaps someone you love as well. You may have gained insights into why you act the way you do, or how any difficulties, disappointments, or frustrations you may have had in your relationships, in your career, or both may be due to insecurity. I hope that you have come away from this book with a better idea of the kind of person you might be looking for in a partner. Finally, if you are a parent you may now have some ideas about how you can promote security in children and how to prevent your child from becoming insecure.

Overcoming insecurity can be a formidable task. So is parenting, especially as we enter this new millennium. We live at a time in which the social fabric seems to be unraveling faster with every passing year.

In order to support people's efforts to understand interpersonal sensitivity, to conquer insecurity, to improve their relationships, and to be better parents, I created the Institute for the Study of Interpersonal Sensitivity (ISIS).

My intention is for ISIS to grow into a resource that will offer opportunities for networking with others who may be struggling with common concerns and issues related to interpersonal sensitivity and insecurity. ISIS is also available as a forum for parents to share common issues as well as their experiences with raising sensitive, secure children.

You are invited to contact ISIS and make use of its resources either via regular mail or via the Internet, through either of the following addresses.

To contact ISIS via standard mail write to:

ISIS
P.O. Box 15
Tolland, Connecticut 06084-0015

To contact ISIS via the World Wide Web, visit the ISIS Web site at www.TheTenderHeart.com.

Acknowledgments

I want to express my appreciation to Linda Konner, writer and agent, for her interest in this project from its inception, and for her good counsel as well. No one could be more ably represented than I have been by Linda.

I also want to acknowledge Betsy Herman, who was intrigued enough to bring *The Tender Heart* to Simon & Schuster. Doris Cooper, editor par excellence, not only contributed energy and enthusiasm; her thoughtful and thorough commentary helped make this a better book.

Thanks to Maggie—daughter, artist, and tender heart—for the use of her artwork for the ISIS Web page, and also for bringing so much joy into my life for so many years.

Last but far from least, thanks to Terri for helping, as always, to bring out the best in me.

About the Author

JOSEPH NOWINSKI, PH.D., is a practicing clinical psychologist and an adjunct associate professor of psychology at the University of Connecticut. The author of seven books and numerous book chapters and articles, he teaches, conducts research, and leads personal growth workshops for individuals and couples, the focus of which is understanding and conquering insecurity, enhancing relationships, and raising sensitive and secure children.

To reach out to others who share his interests, Dr. Nowinski created the Institute for the Study of Interpersonal Sensitivity (ISIS). ISIS provides a means by which men and women communicate with one another, share experiences, and ask questions about interpersonal sensitivity and insecurity. Through its Web site, www.TheTenderHeart.com, ISIS offers forums for professionals, couples, and parents.